I BELIEVE
IN
Miracles

Kathryn Kuhlman

Bridge-Logos
Alachua, Florida

Bridge-Logos

Alachua, FL 32615 USA

I Believe In Miracles
by Kathryn Kuhlman

Copyright ©1962, 1990 by The Kathryn Kuhlman Foundation

All rights reserved. Under International Copyright Law, no part of this publication may be reproduced, stored, or transmitted by any means—electronic, mechanical, photographic (photocopy), recording, or otherwise—without written permission from the Publisher.

Printed in the United States of America.

Library of Congress Catalog Card Number: 92-81626
International Standard Book Number 978-0-88270-657-3

VP 10-08-12

A Message to the readers of this book:

Many of the radio messages by Kathryn Kuhlman are
available on cassette tape, as well as in book form.
If you desire any of her talks, you may request
a listing of subjects by writing to:

The Kathryn Kuhlman Foundation
Post Office Box 3
Pittsburgh, PA 15230

Table of Contents

FOREWORD
Love is Something You Do!

Kathryn Kuhlman is an institution. An ordained minister of the Gospel, she does not consider herself as either a pastor or an evangelist; yet hundreds of people consider her their pastor and few evangelists have the burning passion of this woman, to see lost souls brought out of darkness.

More than fourteen years ago she came to Pittsburgh, Pennsylvania, on a hot Fourth of July day, having rented the auditorium of the Carnegie Library, a city-owned building—the first to have been built by Andrew Carnegie. She has been there ever since.

During the past fourteen years, thousands have packed the same auditorium, not seeking merely the healing of the physical body, but also deliverance from sin and the answer to their problems. Kathryn Kuhlman strongly disapproves of anyone having the idea that this is a ministry devoted only, or even primarily, to the healing of sick bodies. This point she emphasizes in every service—for she believes sincerely that the salvation of the soul is the most important of all miracles. There is no fanaticism in these services: often there is such quietness that the faintest rustle of paper may be heard. Miss Kuhlman attributes this to the fact that the Word of God is the foundation on which she has built her ministry, and she is definite in her belief that if one holds to the Word, there will be *power* without fanaticism.

She has built no building; she has constantly urged those who find salvation in her services to go back to their churches and serve God with all their hearts. For those who have no church home, she is instrumental in building Christian character. When these converts affiliate with a church, they bring to it, by dint of their Spirit-filled witness, a new dynamism.

Kathryn Kuhlman is President of *The Kathryn Kuhlman Foundation,* a religious, charitable, non-profit organization. Her only renumeration is a salary, stipulated by the board of the Foundation.

Seventeen different nationalities are represented in the Foundation's four-hundred-voice Men's Chorus; and the one-hundred-voice Kathryn Kuhlman Concert Choir is considered one of the best in the nation, having been under contract to R.C.A. Victor. The teenage organization is comparable to any youth program of this generation.

The Foundation maintains a Scholarship Fund and a Revolving Loan Fund at Wheaton (Illinois) College, where students in need of financial assistance are being aided in the furthering of their education. The funds are not limited to students majoring in Theology alone, but are available to young men pursuing any secular course of study which the college offers.

The Foundation has been responsible for financing the education of students in Pennsylvania State University, University of Pittsburgh, Carnegie Institute of Technology, Geneva College at Beaver Falls, Pennsylvania; Toccoa Falls Institute in Georgia and College Conservatory of Music in Cincinnati, Ohio.

The Kathryn Kuhlman Foundation has contributed more than forty thousand dollars to the Western Pennsylvania School for Blind Children. Watching a group of little blind children at play one day, struggling with brand-new roller skates, Kathryn Kuhlman became so impressed, so touched, so grateful for her own sight, that she determined that by the grace of God she would do everything humanly possible for these young children.

Dr. Alton G. Kloss, Superintendent of the Western Pennsylvania School for Blind Children, in expressing his appreciation wrote: "Each day as I walk through both our elementary and high school building and our new nursery and kindergarten building, I see your touch. Bright new desks and other comfortable furniture, dishes, draperies, scooters, wagons all attest to the fact that Kathryn Kuhlman has gathered our blind boys and girls into her arms. Your generosity has been a blessing to all of us at the School for Blind Children and your goodness a source of true inspiration."

The Kathryn Kuhlman Foundation has also built and is maintaining an extensive missionary project on Corn Island in South America, just forty miles off the eastern coast of Bluefield, Nicaragua. It was previously known as "Skeleton Island" because it was the last stronghold of the cannibals. With the mother church on the island having been built, plans are underway for scores of outlying stations, which will be pastored by natives who have been trained by other missionaries on the mainland of Nicaragua and here in the United States.

Kathryn Kuhlman's vision has not been so far reaching, that she has forgotten the needy here at home; a poultry dealer received a check for over one thousand, nine hundred dollars for chickens for just one month, which were given to families who needed food. The fowl represented only a small part of the food in the well-stacked baskets. Potatoes come in by the tons and canned goods by cases. There is a well-stocked commissary, where the shelves are constantly replenished with food for those who find themselves in dire circumstances and want. No publicity is ever given to the supplying of food, clothing and assistance to any needy individual or family. This is strictly against Miss Kuhlman's principles. A part of her theology is just this: *Love is something you do!*

Few men work the long hours and have the stamina and vitality of this woman. In connection with her office, the Kathryn Kuhlman Foundation maintains a complete radio studio where work goes on constantly, providing a network of stations with broadcasts which cover two-thirds of the nation weekly.

Miss Kuhlman is heard nightly on Radio Station WWVA, the 50,000-watt station in Wheeling, West Virginia, with reception reaching as far as England; she is no stranger to a large listening audience in Europe. Twice daily she is heard over WADC in Akron, Ohio, from which she receives a tremendous response from Canada. The numbers of letters received each week from listeners in the United States and abroad runs into the thousands.

In spite of her heavy schedule, Miss Kuhlman gives each letter her personal touch, and it is her firm conviction that when she is no longer able to give this part of herself to those who contact her with their burdens and heartaches, then she has failed in her purpose. It is her belief that there are no hopeless situations—there are just folk who have become hopeless about them!

In Kathryn Kuhlman's own words: "I am not a woman with great faith—I am a woman with a little faith in the Great God!"

She was born in Concordia, Missouri, a small town sixty miles from Kansas City, and for several years her father served as mayor. In recalling those early days of her youth, Kathryn says, "Papa was mayor, but in her quiet, reserved and unassuming way, mama helped make many an important decision, as the two sat together on the old-fashioned porch swing."

Religiously, the family was divided: mama was Methodist, for grandpa Walkenhorst was one of the early founders of the Methodist Chuch in Concordia; papa was Baptist, but he never worked too hard at it.

Both her parents are deceased; her father was killed in an accident; her mother died recently.

From the beginning of her evangelistic career, the mission of Kathryn Kuhlman has been to help those who are hungry for Christ to find Him; and from the beginning, the theme of all her sermons has been *faith*.

It was fifteen years ago, in Franklin, Pennsylvania, that members of her congregation suddenly began to claim spontaneous healings during her services. As the number of these healings increased, this Baptist ordained minister began to preach on healing by the Power of God. Thus began today's "Miracle" Services and this unique ministry that has had its influence upon thousands.

The following year Miss Kuhlman moved to Pittsburgh. The fact that she has remained in one location for fourteen years and that her ministry has successfully survived the criticism, which is the lot of all evangelists, is a tribute to her integrity. When asked why she does not extend the scope of her influence by traveling, her reply is: "My purpose is to save souls, and my particular calling is to offer proof of the power of God. I feel I can accomplish this more effectively by staying in one place where I am in a position to follow through on my people, and to insist that those who claim healings procure medical verification." Insistence on scientific substantiation has not only contributed to the soundness of her personal ministry but to spiritual healing everywhere.

SAMUEL A. WEISS

Judge, Court of Common Pleas of Allegheny County
and Former Member of United States Congress

1

I Believe in Miracles

If you are going to read this book "daring" me to convince you of something you do not want to believe, then don't read it. Just forget it! I have neither hope nor expectation of convincing a skeptic simply by miracles.

If you are going to read these pages with a critical, cynical and disbelieving spirit, pass it on for someone else to read; for that which is contained within these pages is very sacred to those to whom these things have happened. Their experiences are too precious and too sacred to be shared with those who would read only to scoff, and listen only to deride. These experiences are guarded in the heart with awe and thanksgiving and deep gratitude. They are as real and wonderful to these people as the moment they happened.

If you believe I am against the medical profession,

against doctors, against the use of medicine because I believe in the power of prayer and the power of God to heal—you are wrong. Had I chosen a profession, in all probability my choice would have been either medicine or law. But I had no choice: I was called of God to preach the Gospel.

At the time the following article was published, Dr. Elmer Hess was president-elect of the American Medical Association. "Any doctor who lacks faith in the Supreme Being has no right to practice medicine," said the Erie, Pennsylvania, specialist in urology. "A physician who walks into a sick room is not alone. He can only minister to the ailing person with the material tools of scientific medicine. His faith in a higher power does the rest. Show me the doctor who denies the existence of the Supreme Being, and I will say that he has no right to practice the healing art."

Hess made these statements in a prepared digest of extemporaneous remarks planned for the opening of the 48th annual meeting of the Southern Medical Association. The SMA, with a total membership of ten thousand doctors, ranks second only to the AMA as the largest general medical organization in the country.

"Our medical schools are doing a magnificent job of teaching the fundamentals of scientific medicine," Hess went on to say. "However, I'm afraid that the concentration on basic science is so great, the teaching of spiritual values is almost neglected."

All healing is Divine, as Dr. Hess so strongly implies. A doctor can diagnose, he can give medication. He can give his patient the best that medical science has given to him and to the world—but in the final analysis, it is the Divine power of God that heals.

A doctor has the power and ability to set a bone, but he must wait for Divine power to heal. A surgeon can skillfully perform the most difficult of operations; he may be a master with a scalpel, using every facet of his well-trained intellect: yet he must wait for a higher power to do the actual healing—for no mere human being has ever been given the power to heal!

Any *truth,* no matter how valid, if emphasized to the *exclusion* of other truths of equal importance, is practical error. My faith in the power of God is the same as that exercised by any physician or surgeon when he believes in the healing and the curing of his patient. He waits for nature (God) to heal gradually, while I believe that God has the ability to heal, not only through a gradual process, but should He so will, His is the ability and the power to heal instantly. He is Omnipotent, Omnipresent and Omniscient: therefore, He is not limited by time nor is He limited by man's ideologies, theologies, and preconceived ideas.

If you believe I think it is a sin to go to a doctor, to take medicine, to have surgery when needed—you do me a great injustice! To be sure, I believe that God has the power to heal instantly without the material tools of scientific medicine; but I *also* believe that God gave us our brains to use! He gave us intelligence—He gave us a will—and he expects us to use good old-fashioned common sense.

If you are ill, and have not yet received the gift of faith so that you believe in miracles, then get yourself the best medical assistance possible, and pray that God shall work through the human vessel: pray that your doctor will be given divine guidance in treating you, and then both of you wait for God to do the actual healing. God's

3

healing power is an indisputable fact, with or without human assistance.

If you believe that I, as an individual, have any power to heal, you are dead wrong. I have had nothing to do with any miracle recorded in this book, nor have I had anything to do with any healing that has taken place in any physical body. I have no healing power whatsoever. All I can do is point you to the way—I can lead you to the Great Physician and I can pray; but the rest is left with you and God. I know what He has done for me, and I have seen what He has done for countless others. What He does for you depends on *you.* The only limit to the power of God lies within the individual!

The exceeding greatness of His power to us-ward who believe, according to His mighty power, which He wrought in Christ, when He raised Him from the dead" (Eph. 1:19).

When God speaks of the greatness of His power, He does not refer to His power which brought the universe into existence, great as that was; but rather to the power which was manifested in raising Jesus from the dead. The Resurrection of Christ was, and our Resurrection with Him *will be,* the greatest demonstration of power—the greatest miracle—which the world has ever known or will ever know.

The Apostle Paul wrote: "If Christ be not risen, then is our preaching vain and your faith is also vain—but now is Christ risen from the dead" (I Cor. 15:14-20).

The validity of the Christian Faith rests on one supreme Miracle: the cornerstone upon which the whole super-structure of Christianity rises or falls, depends on the truth of this Miracle—the Resurrection of Jesus Christ.

4

If this be false, the Apostle Paul confesses that the entire structure falls—for then it is indeed as He says: "Our preaching is vain, and your faith is also vain."

No other religion has ever dared to put forth this challenge; has ever dared to make its appeal *to* miracles, and rest its appeal *on* a Miracle.

Because Christ lives, our faith is not vain—our preaching is not vain; and wonder of wonders is that this exceeding greatness of power is at our disposal. We possess no power of our own; all power belongs to Him!

The fact is, the miracle of the Resurrection of Jesus Christ, the Son of God, is a reality. God has promised the miracle of the Resurrection to these mortal bodies of ours in the future; therefore, it is only reasonable and logical to believe Him for the miracle of healing in our physical bodies today.

If you believe that I do not acknowledge the sacramental methods of healing, used in many different churches, you are under a misapprehension. The power of the Holy Spirit is not confined to any one place or any one system.

We dare not permit ourselves to get so dogmatic in our thinking, our teaching and our methods, that we exclude all other truth of *equal* importance.

For example: We find that God gave the gift of the Holy Spirit on the Day of Pentecost and at the household of Cornelius, without any human agency of "laying on of hands"; but at the Samaritan revival (Acts 8:17) and at the Ephesus revival (Acts 19:6), the believers were filled with the Spirit by the "laying on of hands."

For one to be dogmatic either way, or to make it an issue, is to be guilty of error.

Jesus saw a man who had been born blind, the facts are recorded in the ninth chapter of John. In this particular instance, Jesus spat on the ground, and made clay of the spittle, and He *anointed* the eyes of the blind man with the clay, and said unto him, "Go, wash in the pool of Siloam...he went his way therefore, and washed, and came seeing."

However, on another occasion, as Jesus was nearing Jericho (Luke 18:35), a blind man sat along the roadside begging. In this instance we have no record whatsoever that the hand of the Master ever touched him, and we are sure no clay was put on his eyes. Jesus spoke to the man and said, "Receive thy sight: Thy faith hath saved thee"— and immediately he received his sight.

Both men were blind—both received their sight—different methods were used in each case!

St. James, under the anointing of the Holy Spirit, wrote, "Is any sick among you? Let him call for the elders of the church; and let them pray over him, anointing him with oil in the name of the Lord: and the prayer of faith shall save the sick, and the Lord shall raise him up; and if he have committed sins, they shall be forgiven him" (James 5:14,15).

On the other hand, the power of the Holy Ghost was so great in the early church, "...That they brought forth the sick into the streets, and laid them on beds and couches, that at the least the shadow of Peter passing by might overshadow some of them. There came also a multitude out of the cities round about unto Jerusalem, bringing sick folks, and them which were vexed with unclean spirits: *and they were healed every one*" (Acts 5:15,16). This proves conclusively that the power of the Holy Spirit is not confined to any one place or any one system!

If you believe that I question the spirituality of any minister of the Gospel who does not see eye to eye with me regarding miracles, you are again mistaken, for you misunderstand; our test of fellowship is deeper than the truth concerning healing of the physical body. It is based on something infinitely more important—Salvation through repentance, and faith in the shed blood of Jesus Christ (Hebrews 9:22).

"There is one body, and one Spirit, even as ye are called in one hope of your calling: One Lord, one faith, one baptism, One God and Father of all, who is above all, and through all, and in you all" (Eph. 4:4-6).

All healing is divine, whether it is physical or spiritual; but of the two, it is an undeniable fact, that the spiritual healing is greater.

Nicodemus asked, "How, Master, how can these things be?"

That *is* the mystery which our little minds must leave with God. But this is not the *only* thing you cannot understand, and that you must leave to the knowledge of God.

Explain electricity; or would you rather sit in darkness until you can? Nobody knows exactly what electricity is, yet man does not hesitate to use it just because he does not understand all the laws governing its activity.

Tell me how food is converted into energy in your body. If you do not know, are you refusing to eat?

Tell me how God touches a handful of soil in an uncultivated wooded area, and when he has touched it, the air becomes perfumed with violets.

You paid a dime, the other day, for a package of seeds. For ten cents you purchased a miracle! You have in your possession a dime's worth of something that is known only to God.

In this fast-moving modern day, perhaps we have just overlooked, or taken for granted, miracles that take place every day of our lives.

Tell me what "sets the brain off and causes it to tick"— the great brain surgeons of the medical profession would like to know too. Oh, yes. They know exactly what portion of the brain controls the movement of our every muscle, but they do not know why the brain works as it does; what triggers it into action so that it *can* move and control the various parts of our bodies.

Dr. Charles Joseph Barone, vice-president of the Obstetrical and Gynecological division of the International College of Surgeons, and senior staff doctor of Pittsburgh's Magee Hospital—Pennsylvania's largest maternity hospital—has delivered 25,000 babies. And yet he says, "The birth of a baby is the greatest of miracles."

This physician's training, devotion and dedication to his work have won for him a nation-wide reputation—yet he is the first to admit that human birth is beyond human comprehension: that it is one of the mysteries and sacred things which excite the curiosity and wonderment of man, yet it remains an impenetrable secret.

"Embryological studies of a human cell," says Dr. Barone, "show the markings of the future child—the landmarks that will be the eyes or the heart or the legs or the nose or the lips. If that isn't divine, I don't know what is."

Behold the newborn baby. Nine months ago, he didn't exist. Now he has ears and eyes; a nose and mouth; hands and feet, and a lusty cry when he is hungry. Hours after birth he is feeding happily at his mother's breast.

Did science furnish him with a little xeroxed sheet of instructions, telling him where his dinner was and just how to go about getting it? Was he also told how to close his eyes and sleep, when he was warm and fed? Was he, unable yet even to turn himself over, told how to kick his legs and flail his arms so he would grow strong?

No—no book of instructions was ever given an infant at the moment of his birth. Yet every precious little baby knows exactly what to do to satisfy his wants.

God has never explained to man the secret of physical birth—then why should we hesitate to accept the birth of the spiritual man? Both came from God.

"That which is born of the flesh is flesh, and that which is born of the Spirit is spirit. Marvel not that I said unto thee, ye must be born again" (John 3:6,7).

The spiritual birth gives man a new nature, new desires; the things he once loved, he now hates; and the things he once hated, he now loves, for he is a new creature in Christ Jesus.

How can these things be? When you have the answer to the simple mysteries of which we have spoken and all the many more besides, perhaps God will give you the answer to this last. Until then, keep planting those seeds in your garden, keep using the electricity in your home; and there will continue to be babies born every hour.

With every atom of my being, I pray *you* shall experience the great miracle of the New Birth.

The Bible itself is the greatest of miracles, and the Son

of God more wonderful than any of the wonders that confirm His claims!

The stories that follow are factual; they are the authentic experiences of people who have believed God for a miracle, and God has honored their faith on the authority of His Word. They will help you understand why *I* believe in miracles.

Should you continue with the reading of this book, my prayer shall be that of Paul, when he prayed that the God of our Lord Jesus Christ—"...may give unto you the spirit of wisdom and revelation in the knowledge of Him: the eyes of your understanding, being enlightened" (Eph. 1:17).

2

Carey Reams

"Look Up and Walk"

"MISS KUHLMAN, EVANGELIST, HOLDS HEALING SERVICES HERE, CONVERT TOSSES AWAY CRUTCHES. Climax of the program was reached when a man on crutches, who said he had not walked unaided since 1945, was told to throw away his supports. He did so, and walked briskly up and down the aisles, back and forth across the stage, stretching his leg muscles as he was directed. Beaming, Miss Kuhlman carried his crutches, later casting them aside. The man declared through a loudspeaker that he had heard of Miss Kuhlman in Florida through a magazine article, and had made a special trip alone by bus, to Butler, to attend her services for healing."

These words blazed across the front page of the Butler (Pa.) *Eagle,* January 1, 1951. There was nothing second-hand about this newspaper story.

Evidently the editor of the paper or one of its reporters had sat among the crowd at the Penn Theater the previous day, watching wide-eyed at the marvelous manifestation of the healing power of God.

Carey Reams, the man who had thrown away his crutches, had three children. Only the eldest, four years old when he had gone off to war, thought she could vaguely remember what her father was like before he was almost fatally injured at Luzon during World War II. The other younger children had no recollection of ever seeing their father without crutches. So far as they knew, he had *always* been paralyzed from the waist down, suffering intense pain.

They listened wonderingly to other children talk of how *their* fathers took them on picnics and hikes in the woods and swimming—and knew that for some reason they couldn't understand, their father was different. With legs that couldn't move, he could never take them on any sort of outing. How could he when he couldn't even walk?

Carey Reams was a chemical engineer in the services during World War II. On January 1, 1945, the Allied Forces established a beachhead on Luzon. Carey's unit was ordered to drive toward Manila and free those men who had been captured by the Japanese four years before.

It was a rough assignment. The unit happened to land in a marsh. As Carey says: "There was plenty of water, too, and every time we tried to get out on the highway, we were silhouetted against the sky, and snipers hidden in the mountains would shoot at us. We had to stay in the water the entire first day."

The second day the typhoon started, and the heavens seemed to open as the rains poured down. On the fourth day, Carey's company commander was shot and killed within six feet of him. The commanding officer who immediately replaced him had his own engineer—so Carey was ordered to the next company about six miles away. It was on his way there to report for duty, that it happened. By now the bridge was washed out, and the truck had to go around and over some fill. "It was on this fill," says Carey, "That we hit the land mine. The truck was blown to smithereens."

That was the last Carey knew for a long time.

Thirty-one days later he came to on an operating table, twenty-five hundred miles away from where he had been wounded. He didn't know then where he was or what had happened, but as he regained consciousness, he remembered murmuring—and what he meant he still doesn't know—"I sure did land easy." Immediately after these words were spoken, he was anesthetized for the ensuing brain surgery.

For the next six weeks, Carey floated in and out of consciousness—and then he was shipped home, more dead than alive. He was one of only five survivors in his entire company and, says he, with tears in his eyes, "There would be only *four* of us alive today had I not gotten to that service in the Penn Theater in Butler on that December 31 in 1950."

Carey's remark that he had "landed easily," made when he first regained consciousness, could hardly have been more mistaken.

He had been crushed from the waist through the pelvis; his right eye was gone; he had lost all his teeth; his jawbone was fractured; his neck was broken, and his back was broken in two places. The lower part of his body was completely paralyzed. His legs, like dead weights, hung entirely without sensation, but in those parts of his body in which he still retained feeling, the pain was incredibly intense.

"Any movement there," recalls Carey, "would cause almost deathly agony. And if, for example, my feet got cold, and the blood started to flow back up, it seemed to strike the nerves and the pain was almost unbearable. With no control of my body, and the awful pain, life didn't seem worth living, except for my children. Because of them, I never really wanted to die—and I wouldn't give up."

At the same time, Carey was suffering hemorrhage after hemorrhage and had lost sixty pounds in weight.

Before his healing in Butler, he had been operated on some forty-one times. He was all too familiar with the inside of hospitals—two overseas—then Letterman General Hospital in California—a hospital in Georgia—and in the five years prior to his healing, he had been repeatedly hospitalized in the Veterans Administration Hospital in Florida.

Although Carey's body was in such shocking condition, his mind was clear as crystal, and as he says, "I see now that God was taking care of me all along"; for many people who knew that Carey was a good engineer and could not go out on the job, brought him their engineering problems and blueprints—and although he couldn't walk a step, and for many, many months could not even leave his bed, he was thus able to support his family.

By December of 1950, however, he was in desperate straits physically. He was now virtually unable to eat food of any kind; he was suffering repeated hemorrhages, and his life was slowly but surely ebbing out.

"You know," he says, "sometimes we just have to hold on when there is nothing to hold on to—and I was at that point. I was just hanging on to life by a thread."

It was a few days before Christmas when the local Veterans Administration doctor ordered Carey back to Bay Pines, the Veterans Administration Hospital near St. Petersburg.

"These Veterans Administration doctors are wonderful," says Carey, "and I can't praise them and the wonderful government hospitals enough. They give you the very best that science has to offer. But this time I refused to go. I remember saying, 'No, doctor, if I'm going to die, I want to spend this last Christmas with my family. It's only a question now of a few days until the holidays. After Christmas you can do whatever you want with me.'

It was during these few days," Carey continued, "that I happened to read an article about Kathryn Kuhlman in a national magazine. At the same time, I received letters from three different friends telling me about the healing services in Pittsburgh. These friends had written to ask me why I didn't try to get to Pittsburgh to one of her services.

"Pittsburgh, Pennsylvania, did not seem so remote to me, for my wife was from Pittsburgh, and I also knew Clyde Hill, a driver for the Yellow Cab Company. The thought flashed through my mind that perhaps I could stay with my friend, should I decide to make the trip. The more I thought about it, the more I realized that getting to a miracle service was my last and only hope."

The big question was, how to get there? Not only was Carey paralyzed, but he was so weak from loss of blood through hemorrhaging that he could hardly sit up. He didn't feel physically able to ride to Pittsburgh under any circumstances. If he attempted the trip, he knew one of two things would happen; he would either die before he could return to Florida—or he would be healed. "But," as he puts it, "I finally decided that God hadn't kept me hanging on to life by a thread for so long for nothing. I truly believed that He would heal me if I could just get to Pittsburgh—and that when I was well, He would give me something to do for Him."

On December 28, early on a Thursday morning, Carey, all alone, painfully and slowly climbed aboard a bus bound for Pittsburgh. Approximately thirty-six hours later he arrived at Carnegie Hall to attend the Friday miracle service. At the doors he was delivered a crushing blow: the service had been dismissed an hour before. He never dreamed the service had started at nine o'clock in the morning!

Totally exhausted; on the verge of collapse from weakness so that even with the aid of crutches he could scarcely stand; and in almost intolerable pain, he only wondered if he could hold out for the next two days, when his friend, the cab driver, would take him to the Sunday service scheduled to be held in Butler, Pennsylvania.

Throughout the next forty-eight hours, he had only one thought in mind—to hang on to life till he could get to the Butler Meeting. This was the determination—the faith, that God in His tender mercy would please give him the strength to live long enough to get to the Penn Theater at Butler on December 31, 1950.

He almost didn't make it. With less than twenty-four hours to go, he suffered another extraordinarily severe hemorrhage—which left him so weak he could not get up or walk without the help of two strong men. With their assistance he arrived at the Penn Theater.

At the door almost all hope left him, for he was told that all seats were taken, there was no more room inside. There he stood, clinging to his crutches, supported by two men, in the freezing outside temperature. So near and yet so far—so weak that every minute seemed an hour.

Just as he was about to give up the last vestige of hope, someone inside who had noted his predicament, offered him her seat. "I have *been* healed," she said. Grateful beyond words, he entered the theater.

Did he feel the glory of God the moment he walked in?

"Not just at first," he smiles in recollection, "I was in so much pain when I first came in that for the first few minutes I couldn't even think of anything else, but a little later I was to know Him as I had never known Him before."

"Just as I was being seated," recalls Carey, "Miss Kuhlman began to speak. The first thing she said was, 'The meeting this afternoon is a soul-searching meeting and not one for healing.' "

If Mr. Reams had thought his hope was on the bottom rung of the ladder earlier, he found now that there was still another rung to go. There he sat, half frozen, so weak he had to use his crutches for braces to sit up, and he heard me say that this meeting was not for healing!

"I thought then I was dying physically," Carey says, "but now I know that I was only dying to self."

"It was a wonderful sermon," he continued in recollection, "and blessed everyone but me. I had traveled over one thousand miles to be healed; the meeting was coming to a close, and I had not been healed."

Many souls had been saved that day, more than fifty

men had responded to the altar call, and many marvelous healings had been received, but Carey Reams was not among those healed. He was cruelly disappointed and was filled with utter despair.

The strains of the last hymn had just died away, and the theater was so quiet you could have heard a pin drop. In Carey's words: "Miss Kuhlman raised her hand for a benediction, but she didn't speak a word, and my heart sank. At that moment all my hope was gone. Then, very slowly her hand came down and she looked directly at me, and pointing a finger straight at me she said, 'Are you from Florida?' My hopes soared as I replied, 'Yes.' Then," Carey went on, "she asked me to stand up and I said, 'I can't—and she said, firmly, 'IN THE NAME OF JESUS, STAND UP AND LOOK UP, AND WALK!' "

Carey started to get up on his crutches. The aisles were narrow, and he had on a big, heavy overcoat. It was ten degrees below zero that day in Butler, and coming from Florida, he wasn't used to cold like that. Attempting to get down that narrow aisle, bundled in an overcoat, paralyzed and manipulating crutches on a slanty floor— trying not to step on people's feet. It was no mean task to *look up,* but somehow he managed to achieve it.

"All of a sudden," relates Carey, "Miss Kuhlman said: 'Take that right crutch away.' I tried it and it worked: my leg bore my weight—and I remember being amazed how she *knew* this would be the case."

At that moment the pain in his body instantly vanished. "It was like a light going out," Carey described, "or like ink spreading on a blotter."

Realizing that his one leg was successfully bearing his

weight, Carey dropped the second crutch and stood alone and unaided.

"Miss Kuhlman then told me to come up on the platform," very steep—about twelve of them in all. Two big, strong gentlemen stepped up to my side to help me, but I didn't need any help. I walked onto the platform like a bird flying up. I seemed hardly to touch the floor, and I didn't *walk* toward Miss Kuhlman, I *ran.*"

Was he surprised at his healing? "No, I was not," he replies in firm tone. "This is what I came for."

Was he amazed when he found himself walking without crutches? "No, I was not," he responds. "I *expected* to walk without them."

And this is the answer.

"On that first day, Miss Kuhlman told me to look up," Carey Reams says with a smile—"and I've been looking up ever since, in praise and thanksgiving to God..."

The day after his healing, Carey borrowed a little over a hundred dollars from his friend, Clyde, using most of it for payment in full on a second-hand truck. He needed a truck to take his wife's furniture, which was in storage in Pittsburgh back to Florida. That afternoon he helped load the truck with furniture, and drove it back to Florida!

A man, helpless and dying, was touched by the Great Physician—instantly healed, and the next day loaded a truck with furniture and drove all the way from Pittsburgh, Pennsylvania, to Florida. This is God, and Carey Reams is a living testimony to His power.

Three days later he drove into his own garage in Florida—and walked unannounced into the living room of his home where his three children were playing.

All three children looked up and gasped as he strode

into the room. They sat motionless for several seconds—they could not believe their own eyes, for this was the first time in their lives that the two youngest children had ever seen their father walking without his crutches. Then, suddenly, the full realization of what had happened came upon them—their daddy could walk—their daddy was healed, and as Carey put it, "They all began to *chirp*. Only children filled with glee can make that peculiar chirrup sound—like happy birds."

Half-laughing and half-crying, they jumped up and down and clapped their little hands, and then just *looked*.

"I was just so happy, I couldn't do anything but watch them and rejoice," Carey continued. "I hadn't realized that *my* rejoicing would go any further than myself, and that the children really cared so much. But my, how they *did* rejoice that night! I only wish I had a picture of the joy and wonder on their faces as they saw me stand there without crutches, and then walk across the room to them."

From that time to this, and it has been eleven years now, Carey has been the picture of perfect, robust health. Able to walk and to run and to climb, there remains no indication whatsoever of his former paralysis.

With seventeen dollars left of the money he had borrowed from the cab driver—with this as his sole capital, he went into business for himself. From the very beginning, this business thrived. Carey is a Consultant Agricultural Engineer, and only recently he was a candidate for Commissioner of Agriculture for Florida.

He owns his own home now, and gives infinitely more than the biblical tithe to religious work. Every penny over and above what is absolutely essential for simple living, he gives away in order to train youths in Christian education.

Why is he tirelessly giving of his time and effort to the religious education of youth?

"Because," he says, "statistics show that seventy-five percent of the boys and girls trained in religious schools become, as adults, active church workers and churchgoers, while only twenty-five per cent without this kind of education, end up going to church. When we realize three out of four trained in church school are Christians, stay Christians, and raise a Christian family, it seems a most important thing in and for the world to see that these youngsters get that kind of training."

There were some in the auditorium the day that Carey Reams was healed, who had difficulty in believing what they saw, so spectacularly dramatic it was.

I, myself, had never seen Mr. Reams before; he had come from a great distance and I knew nothing about him. To allay any doubts as to the truth of his healing, I had his background carefully looked into.

He was given excellent character references by all who knew him, including several judges. His previous condition was found to be exactly as he had claimed it, and his medical records are on file in the hospitals as he has stated. His healing is an indisputable miracle, wrought by an all-powerful and all-merciful God.

Carey Reams' only son is now a senior in high school. He has a daughter who is studying to be a nurse, and his "baby" is thirteen years old. These are the children who did the "chirping" that January evening eleven years ago.

"Every night we have our family devotions. The children love you and will never forget you. They never hush talking about Miss Kuhlman." Greater appreciation I have never seen on the face of a man, than was expressed on the face of Mr. Reams as he spoke those words.

I replied swiftly what I believed: that this is simply because they are so grateful to Jesus for what He did for their daddy.

I urged him once again, to emphasize to his children that I had nothing to do with his healing. Such miracles are *always* due to the power of the Holy Spirit and to His power alone. There is one thing God will not share with any human being, and that is the "glory."

"For thine is the kingdom, and the power, and the glory, forever" (Matt. 6:14).

3

Stella Turner
Sent Home to Die!

Herbert Turner was not emotional by temperament, but any husband is nervous when his wife is undergoing surgery, and Herbert was no exception. As he paced back and forth waiting for news from the doctors, the strain he was undergoing was very apparent.

He had glanced at his watch a thousand times, wondering how long it took to remove a gall bladder, when finally he saw approaching him the two operating surgeons. One look at their downcast faces flooded him with fear. Before he had time to question them, one spoke, "I'm terribly sorry to have to tell you this, Mr. Turner, but your wife has cancer."

Stunned for a moment, Herbert was silent-and then he asked, "Where—*where* is the cancer? Did you get it all out?"

The surgeon shook his head—and then as gently as possible, explained, "It's all through her body—liver; stomach; gall bladder; pancreas. It is so widespread and she is so far gone, that we couldn't operate."

"How long does she have?" Herbert asked in a voice that seemed to belong to someone else.

"Six to eight weeks," was the answer. "She'll be able to leave the hospital in nine or ten days. Then all you can do is keep her comfortable till the end comes."

It seemed to Herbert that at that moment, his world collapsed.

Herbert Turner, who worked for the Internal Revenue Department in Massillon, Ohio, had been worried over his wife for months. He had watched her weight drop from 132 pounds to 97. He had watched her growing inability to eat, until finally she could not even retain gruel on her stomach—and he had watched her increasingly frequent bouts of almost unbearable pain.

When she had entered the hospital on that 25th day of January in 1952, he couldn't help but wonder if a malfunctioning gall bladder were responsible for *all* her troubles. And now the surgeon, one of the five present at the operation, had confirmed his worst fears. Stella, at 49 years of age, was being sent home to die.

"Are you going to tell her the truth?" Herbert asked. The doctor shook his head.

"We won't tell her anything right away," he said. "When the full report comes back from the pathologist, we'll tell her she has a malignant tumor which we could not remove at this time."

When they told her just this several days later, the patient wasn't fooled for an instant. She was fully aware of the implications that having an inoperable tumor suggest.

Stella was due to return home on Sunday, after nine days in the hospital.

It was very late the Wednesday night before—and Herbert, his daughter and sister-in-law sat at home, after their evening visit to the hospital. They sat in silence— grief-stricken over Stella's impending, and apparently inevitable death. Then suddenly Stella's sister said: "Let's all write in a prayer request to Kathryn Kuhlman."

Seeing Herbert's puzzled expression, his sister-in-law explained that a friend of hers had told her about the services and the broadcasts.

"Medicine can't help her, now," she reminded Herbert. "Perhaps this will."

Herbert was a regular churchgoer, as was his wife—and he believed in prayer—but neither one of them had ever heard of divine healing. "We thought this was something that had just occurred in biblical times," he says. "We never knew it was going on *now*."

As he listened to his sister-in-law tell about the Friday Miracle Services, Herbert exclaimed, "Then what are we waiting for? If we send in a prayer request tonight, it will get there in time for the service on Friday."

Thus they wrote out the request, and at three A.M. Herbert took it down to the railroad station to mail.

"I was desperate," Mr. Turner says. "I knew the only thing we could pin our hopes on now was God. I believed in the power of prayer, and if it were true that God still heals today, I figured that if all those believing people at Carnegie Hall were to pray for Stella, something just *might* happen."

Stella did not know when she left the hospital two days after the Miracle Service, of the prayer request sent in on her behalf. She believes now, however, in view of what happened, that her healing actually began at daybreak on that Sunday in the hospital, for at that time, at ten-minute intervals and continuing for thirty-six hours, her bowels moved; "carrying the poison out of my body," she says.

Stella's condition after she got home seemed to follow exactly the prediction of her doctors; but her husband and daughter—and she herself after she learned of divine healing and began to listen to the broadcasts—stood firm in the face of her adverse physical manifestations. They held a faith that nothing would shake, that she would be healed.

She was almost entirely bedridden—too weak and too sick to be out of bed except for very brief periods of time. The pain was intolerable without generous doses of the pain-killing drugs the doctors had sent home with her. "When these are gone," they had said at the hospital, handing her a slip of paper, "Ask your husband to get this prescription filled."

Stella did not know until much later that her sister and two nephews were going regularly to the services to pray for her. She herself was taken to her first service about six weeks after she had gotten home from the hospital.

So sick was she then, that she wondered if she would survive the trip to Youngstown. She vomited all the way there—and far too weak to walk, her husband and son-in-law had to practically carry her up the steps of Stambaugh Auditorium, for she did not weigh much more than ninety pounds.

"I felt the Presence that first time," Stella says; "and I experienced the power."

Every Sunday thereafter, no matter how sick she was, they made the trip into Youngstown. Although she was not instantaneously healed, her condition began to slowly improve. She had been unable to eat more than a few teaspoons of gruel for months, but on the way back home after the third Sunday, she asked that her husband stop and buy some fresh vegetables. He remonstrated: "You can't eat anything like *that!*"

"Yes I can," she said, "I *know* I can." And that night she ate a large platter of vegetables without ill effect.

The following week, she asked her husband to stop for dinner in Youngstown; there she consumed the first meal she had been able to eat and enjoy since her illness had begun.

There was no doubt that she was definitely improving, but her pain continued. One night in early May, she ran out of the drugs the hospital had given her, and she asked her husband to go to the drugstore and get the prescription filled.

"I walked into that drugstore," Herbert said, "and suddenly it was as if I heard a voice say, 'Stella's not going to need these pain pills.' I just turned around and walked out again, the prescription still in my hand."

That prescription was never filled. From that day on, Stella never needed another pain-killing drug. Within a period of months, she had completely regained her strength, and as her husband said: "From that time on she has been able to do more work than any two other women I know; scrubbing walls—cutting the grass. In the beginning I just couldn't keep her from working!"

27

Yes, the skeptic may say, but cancer is a disease which often has remissions. How do you know that this has not happened in Stella's case? How do you know beyond any doubt that today there is no cancer in this woman's body?

On June 1, 1955, three and one-half years after her cancer healing, she became ill, and her doctor once again diagnosed gall bladder trouble. *She* wasn't the least bit worried, for by now she knew that those whom God has healed, *stay* healed; and her husband and daughter shared her faith.

She returned to the same hospital, to the same team of surgeons who had taken care of her before.

But this time things were very different when the doctors came down from the operating room to give Herbert the news. Again he watched them approach him—the same two as before. As they drew near, he observed their expression, and again he knew what to expect. But this time their countenances were not grim and downcast, but a curious mixture of jubilation and bewilderment.

"Well—?" Herbert asked.

"No cancer," came the reply.

"How do you explain this?" asked Herbert, anxious to hear what they would say.

"There is only one way to explain it," they answered. "Someone higher than ourselves took care of your wife."

Where the cancer had been, there was now nothing except scar tissue. Where previously the organs had been damaged, they were now fully restored and in perfect condition. There was no physical sign of active cancer in Stella Turner's body.

As before, they had biopsies done in the Massillon City Hospital laboratory, to confirm their diagnosis, but in view of the circumstances this time, they also sent sections for examination to Columbus, Ohio. The reports came back negative.

Had the original diagnosis been mistaken?

No—not one of the doctors claimed this—for *five* surgeons had assisted at the first operation and had seen with their own two eyes the condition of Mrs. Turner's body.

Some may wonder why she had to have this second operation three and one-half years after her healing of cancer. I believe it was to give proof positive that the cancer was no longer there. Only surgery could give this proof to those who might have doubts.

Stella recovered from the gall bladder operation with a rapidity which further amazed her doctors. When she returned to her family physician a month later for a check-up, he put his arm around her and said, "I'm so happy for you. You and your family are a living example to all of us as to what faith can do."

The lives of the Turners are very different since Stella's healing. They are closer together as a family than they had ever been before, and each one of them lives close to God. They attend the services, as well as their own church, regularly. Stella never misses a broadcast, and while for years Herbert could only listen on holidays, he has now retired and they listen together each day, on their knees in prayer, and with thanksgiving. They read their Bibles daily, and witness far and wide to the power of God in their lives.

The husband—the wife—the doctors—the preacher lady; not one of us knows what happened or how. We only know that God did it—and this is all we have to know.

O Jesus, we stand amazed in your presence. We cannot

tell how these things are done. We cannot analyze the workings of the Holy Spirit. We only know that by your power these miracles are wrought—and so long as we live, we shall give you the praise and the honor and the glory.

4

George Orr
"This is Really Something!"

It was Sunday morning. For thousands of people, it was just another Sunday, but for George Orr it was to prove one of the most unusual and thrilling days of his life.

Twenty-one years and five months prior to this day, George had suffered an accident in the foundry where he worked in Grove City, Pennsylvania.

Countless times during the years in which George had worked in the foundry, he had followed the same routine without mishap. Filling a comparatively small ladle from the vat of molten iron next to the cupola (furnace), he and two other men would carry the ladle back to the area in which they were working at the time, and pour it into the molds to be cast that day.

On the morning of December 1, 1925, they had to carry it a little farther than usual. On the return trip to the furnace, they saw that there was a small amount of the metal still remaining in their ladle. They hurried, then, before it solidified, to pour it back into the large container, already almost full to capacity with its new load of molten metal. As they poured, and the iron fell in, it splashed.

"I saw it coming," says George, "and instinctively closed my eyes." But an eyelid is no protection against red-hot liquid iron. It burned through the eyelid and lay inside his eye—just cooking it," as he puts it.

In excruciating pain, George was rushed to the nearby company nurse, who quickly removed the now solid splinter of metal, which was the size of a large grain of wheat. George was sent immediately to an eye specialist who quickly administered a pain-killing drug—and then shook his head as he said, "I'm sorry, Orr, but you'll never see out of this eye again."

Six months of suffering lay ahead for George.

The eye quickly became infected in spite of the precautionary treatment. For six long months the suffering was so intense that he could not lie in bed. He slept, when he was able to, on the floor of the living room so he would not disturb the rest of the family.

During the next year George consulted a number of doctors, including an outstanding eye specialist in Butler, Pennsylvania. The latter, after examining the injured eye, had him admitted to the hospital where, after exhaustive examination, the final verdict was rendered: he would never see again out of his right eye. Subsequently, in 1927, he was awarded workmen's compensation by the state of Pennsylvania for the industrial injury—the loss of his eye.

It was bad enough to lose his vision in *one* eye, but

gradually as time went on he began to notice, to his distress, that the other eye was going bad. He experienced more and more difficulty in reading—and "long before it got really dark in the evening," he recalls, "I would have to stop what I was doing simply because I couldn't see. I never said anything to my family, but they knew, as I did, that my sight was going."

George then went to an eye specialist in Franklin, Pennsylvania—at that time one of the outstanding eye specialists in the country. The doctor explained what was happening: the sightlessness of his right eye, the cornea covered with heavy scar tissue, had cast too heavy a burden on his once "good" eye. Regardless of glasses, it was hopelessly overtaxed by the necessity of carrying the full load of vision.

George inquired again about the possibility of surgery to remove the scar tissue from his injured eye, but again the reply was negative: the scar tissue went too deep to remove. Haunting George now was the specter of eventual total blindness.

It was early in 1947 that the Orr's eldest daughter, living in Butler, told her father of the broadcasts she had heard over the radio, and suggested that he and her mother go to one of the services.

In March they attended their first service.

"I wasn't completely sold that first time," says George. "I knew there were many preaching divine healing who were not all they should be, and I was on guard. I had to be sure about this ministry before I could go all the way along with it."

That evening, he and his wife talked the service over at great length. George did a lot of thinking as they talked, and finally he said, "You know, I'm sure that Kathryn Kuhlman has something. I want to go back again—and next time I do, I'll really enter into the service."

During the next two months, they went back several times, and George says, "My doubts were all removed when I saw the scope and depth of this ministry. I knew it was the real thing."

The fourth day of May was a Sunday—and the Orrs had company. Two of their married children and their families were there, and they had planned a festive Sunday dinner for around one o'clock.

Just at noon, friends of the Orrs stopped by—a young couple who were on their way to the service.

"We thought you'd probably like to come along with us, George. How about it?" they asked.

"No," said George, "We have company and we haven't had dinner yet. And besides," he added, "It's too late; we'd never get seats."

But his children, knowing that if they were not there, their father would have gone to the service, insisted that both their parents go, and the Orrs finally agreed.

Getting in their friends' car, with the young husband driving, they started off.

They arrived after the service had already begun. The hall was packed, and they had resigned themselves to standing for the next three and a half or four hours, when one of them saw in the fourth row, center section, four seats all together.

"It seemed as if those seats were just there waiting for *us,*" George says. "We just walked in the front door and sat down."

There were a great many who were healed that day, but

George apparently was not to be among them. "And then," he says, "Miss Kuhlman made a statement I had never heard before. She said that *healing* was there for everyone just as *salvation* was. 'That's it!' I thought, so I said, 'God, please heal my eye.' I didn't ask for both eyes."

And that *was* it for George Orr. Immediately upon asking to be healed, the blinded eye began to burn intensely. Although he had the faith that God was going to heal that eye, George did not grasp at once the significance of what was happening.

His upper eyelid having been burned out at the time of the accident, was in a V-shape. Often when he lowered his eyelashes, they would strike the eyeball and cause pain and a burning sensation. This is what George thought had happened now, but then he noticed that the woman sitting next to him was staring at the front of his coat. He looked down to see what she was looking at and saw that it was soaking wet, with the tears streaming from his blinded eye.

"I remember how terribly embarrassed I was," smiles George, "and how quickly I took out my handkerchief and wiped off my jacket."

The meeting was dismissed, and as George got out of his seat and tried to walk down the aisle, he found that he could not walk straight. He turned to the young man with whom he had come, and said, "I have the strangest feeling. I can't explain it, but something has come over me which I don't understand.

It was the power of God, which he had never before experienced.

The two couples started back to Grove City.

"When we made the turn into our route," relates George, "I noticed the marking on the road—Routes 8 and 62. I had never seen these signs before, but I *still* didn't realize what had happened.

"We went clear over the hill," George continues, "and suddenly it seemed as though a heavy cloud which had covered the sun, all at once passed over, and the sun came out very bright and strong. I looked up into the sky, but there was no cloud anywhere in sight."

George realized then that something tremendous had happened.

They were at that moment on a section of the hill where a road approach below was visible. George closed his "good" eye and with his other—blind for over twenty-one years—he could see the cars going up the other hill.

"I was dumbstruck," he says in recollection. "I couldn't believe it, and I didn't say anything for a good while. I felt completely overwhelmed by the wonder of it."

And then he finally turned to his wife and exclaimed, "I can *see!* I can see *everything!*"

When they arrived home, George entered the house in an unaccustomed way. The plan of the house is such that one enters through the hall into the kitchen. But on this day, George went through the living room, through the dining room, to the back door.

"Clear across the floor in the kitchen," he says, "was a small clock I had bought, one of those wall clocks with a very small face. Before I turned to face the clock, my wife said, "What time is it by that clock? Can you *really* see with that eye?"

George covered the other eye, and read the dial: "Quarter to six," he replied without hesitation.

His wife smiled, her face joyful, and said, "Oh, thank God, it's true. You *can* see!"

You will note that I had never prayed for George Orr; I had never touched him. His healing came to him as, unknown to me, he sat in the auditorium that May afternoon in 1947.

George went back to the office of the optometrist who over twenty-one years before had made the glasses for his "good" eye. He found that the man he had known was dead, but his successor was in his place. George asked him to examine his eye, but before he did so, George said, "This eye has quite a history."

"Well, let's hear it," came the answer.

But before he told of his experience, George asked a question: "Do you believe in divine healing?"

"Yes," was the reply. "I do."

Then George knew that he was free to talk and related what happened to him.

The optometrist made a thorough examination, in the middle of which he asked, "Where did you get your last glasses?"

When George replied; "Right here in this office," the optometrist said, "Then your records must be here. Wait a minute."

He went back to the inner office, and came out with the records. He studied them, and as he read, he kept looking up at George in a puzzled way.

He then replaced the records and completed his examination. He said, "Mr. Orr, the scar on your right eye has completely disappeared." And then he went on to ask, "Did you know what extremely bad condition your *other* eye was in the last time it was examined?"

George, remembering all too well his fear of total blindness, nodded.

"Well," the optometrist said, "You have received a marvelous healing not only in one, but in *both* your eyes!"

About two years after his healing, George decided to play a little trick on the doctor who had taken care of him in Butler, both while he was in the hospital, and after he had gotten out; the same doctor who had submitted his findings to the compensation board—findings which resulted in state compensation for the loss of an eye.

"I knew he wouldn't remember me after all these years," said George, "So I took Mrs. Orr along with me and in my pocket I put a slip of paper: the referee's award of compensation—and then I walked into the doctor's office and asked him to examine my eye!"

After the examination, George asked, "Well, how do you find me?"

"In excellent shape," the physician said, "One eye is slightly better than the other, but that's nothing. My eyes are exactly the same way. Your left eye is perfect: the right has 85 per cent normal vision."

With that, George reached into his pocket and handed him the findings of the board of compensation.

The doctor read it in astonishment, and kept on repeating, "This is *something*—this is *really* something."

He made no attempt to deny the healing—he couldn't—for the record was there in front of him.

A miracle was wrought by God in the life of George Orr.

"Lord, that I might receive my sight!" had been his supplication. And as to the blind Bartimaeus nearly two thousand years ago, had come the answer: "Go thy way; thy faith hath made thee whole" (Mark 10:52).

5

Eugene Usechek

"I Heard the Voice of God..."

The handsome young man walked proudly into Children's Hospital in Pittsburgh. He was going there by appointment to see a well-known doctor. This was a very momentous occasion in his life, for he was going to take his physical before his entrance into the United States Air Force.

He was returning to the same doctor who had been his physician when he was afflicted with Perthe's disease at the age of nine.

None of the Usechek family will ever forget that year when Eugene, the oldest of their three sons, was nine.

On the day after Christmas, 1949, Mrs. Usechek had gone into town to take advantage of the after-Christmas sales. She left Eugene and his younger brothers in the care of a sixteen-year old boy, who had often watched them in the past when she wanted to be away for a few hours.

When she got home late that afternoon, the boys greeted her with their usual high spirits and prattled away about the fun they had had with their "baby sitter"—especially about the good game he and Eugene had played—a sort of tug-of-war with a strap tied around their legs, seeing who could pull the hardest.

Whether this was in any way responsible for what happened, no one will ever know, but two days later Eugene began to limp.

Mrs. Usechek asked him if his leg hurt, and when he said no, she didn't worry. Anyone who knows small boys, knows how continually they roughhouse and engage in horseplay—so Eugene's mother naturally assumed that her son had a bruise on his leg.

But he continued to limp, and after several weeks she grew concerned when it appeared to be getting definitely worse. She took him then, over his protestations ("But nothing hurts, mom!") to their family doctor who promptly came to the same conclusion that Mrs. Usechek had earlier: that it was doubtless just a bruise.

Two weeks later, however, Eugene came home from school one day, complaining that his left heel hurt. His mother examined the foot carefully, but could find no sign of an injury.

For the next few days, Eugene complained more and more about the pain in his heel. His mother noticed that he seemed to be favoring it—at least he never let it touch the ground.

She took him again to the family doctor, who ordered X-rays. Two days later, with deep concern in his voice, the physician rendered the verdict: Eugene was a victim of

Perthe's disease. To Mrs. Usechek's worried question, the doctor explained that this is a disease in which changes take place in the bone at the head of the femur (thigh bone) which results in the deformity. He urged her to make an immediate appointment with an eminent orthopedist at Children's Hospital.

Within a few days, Eugene and his mother were sitting in the specialist's office.

The physician examined the boy carefully, and then called in another orthopedist for consultation. They conferred for a few minutes together, and then told Mrs. Usechek that her son must be admitted at once to the hospital. They pointed out something she had not noticed before—that the boy's left leg was underdeveloped compared to his right, and was already a good one and a half inches shorter.

During the ten days in the hospital, more X-rays were taken; the diagnosis was confirmed beyond any shadow of doubt, and the boy was placed in traction. This had no effect on the shortened limb, and he was placed in a cast from his chest to his toes, and released from the hospital.

This was in February, and four months later he returned to the hospital where the cast was removed and more X-rays taken. He was then placed in another cast, which was to remain on until August.

It was late in June that Mrs. Usechek first heard of the services being held in Carnegie Hall.

"A neighbor advised me to listen to the broadcast," she said, "and then send in my prayer request. The very next day I began to listen, and started to fast and pray for Eugene's healing."

On August 1, she took her son back for more X-rays. The cast was now removed, and a brace was substituted.

It had been bad enough to be in a cast during the blistering hot weather that summer, but the brace, also extending from the boy's hips to his toes and weighing fifteen pounds, proved even more uncomfortable. Eugene, incredibly patient during this whole period, never complaining, even attempting to play baseball with the "gang" while in his cast and on crutches, now pleaded with his mother: "Mommy, please, can't I have the cast back instead of this brace?"

This plea of her little son, broke his mother's heart—particularly in view of the fact that he might well have to wear such a brace for the rest of his life, and that his leg, unless touched by God, would very probably grow progressively worse, continuing as it had already begun, to shrivel into complete uselessness and deformity.

On the last of August, she went alone to her first service at Carnegie Auditorium.

"I had only been to my own church and never seen a religious service like this," smiled Mrs. Usechek, "and I had never even heard of the new birth experience.

"I liked the service, but I didn't understand anything about it. Even so, I felt something in that auditorium that I had never felt before, and I wanted to go back and learn more about it."

The following week Mrs. Usechek took Eugene—brace and all. Other people were wonderfully healed that day, but not Eugene. As Mrs. Usechek says, "I was still very ignorant about the whole thing. It was all so very new to me."

In early October of 1950, Mrs. Usechek took Eugene again to Carnegie Hall. They were a little late getting to the service, and could not find a seat, so they stood back against the far wall of the auditorium. And suddenly it happened. Eugene's left leg began to twitch—the power of God was going through it.

Mrs. Usechek looked quickly at her son, and saw the radiance in his face. She held her child close and started to cry. Then she suddenly realized that what remained to be done now was between her and God. She would have to have the faith to believe God to the point of action—her action. She said a quick prayer, and before it was finished, she knew she had been given that faith.

With her little boy's hand in hers, Mrs. Usechek took him to the ladies' lounge. She told him to wait there for a moment, and she went out to find an usher. The first one she saw, she stopped and asked for a screwdriver. He managed to get one for her quickly; and she thanked him and took it into the lounge.

There, with a prayer on her lips, she unscrewed and took off the brace from her little boy's built-up left shoe. Then she had him take off both shoes and asked him to walk across the spacious lounge. He did so without difficulty and without any sign of a limp. She then stood him before her, and saw what had happened: the left leg had miraculously lengthened the lacking one and a half inches and was exactly the same as the right!

They walked home together, Mrs. Usechek carrying the brace.

The next morning she called the doctor and he was completely horrified to hear what she had done. He told her that removal of the brace would do her son incalculable harm, taking from him any hope that there might be of any future improvement.

Mrs. Usechek was frankly terrified, and during the next few weeks she engaged in the most terrible inner conflict she had ever endured.

She had acted in and by faith. She completely believed in the power of God to heal; she knew that God had touched Eugene. But then, she told herself, God works through doctors, too. Perhaps she should pay attention to what the doctors were telling her.

During those next few weeks she put the brace back on and took it off, as she says, at least a thousand times. After talking to the doctors, she would put it on, and after earnest prayer, she would take it off.

One day, almost immediately after she had put it on, the leg broke out in boils.

"This was God speaking," she says, "and I know it now, but then I was just too upset and uncertain and frightened to listen."

She took it off then, until the boils cleared up, and then she put it back on. This time the leg almost at once, and for no discernible reason, turned black and blue.

"Finally," she says, "I heard the voice of God and saw His hand in these things. I took it off once and for all and kept it off. Having made up my mind to *really* believe God for Eugene's healing, I stopped being afraid."

His leg, from the moment she first took the brace off in the auditorium twelve years ago, has remained perfect.

At the request of his doctors, Mrs. Usechek took Eugene back at regular intervals for check-ups. They were astonished at his healing, and conceded that it was a miracle.

Three years after the healing, she was to receive what is now one of her most treasured possessions: a letter dated March, 1953, and signed by both the eminent orthopedists who had treated her son. They asked that she bring Eugene back to the hospital and offered to pay any expenses involved—so that he might help others *without* faith to believe, and to prove to them that the healing power of God was real.

Mr. and Mrs. Usechek donated the brace which their son had worn for so short a time before his healing to the hospital.

Eugene attended Waynesburg College, where he played on the baseball team, and won the trophy for the outstanding wrestler in his class.

And then he decided he wanted to join the United States Air Force, where the physical requirements are probably stricter than in any other field of endeavor in the United States.

Before they accepted him in October, 1961, they had him go back to the same doctors who had treated him for Perthe's disease and have an X-ray taken.

He is now a member of the Air Force, serving in the Secret Code Division.

After hearing this story of God's power, who cannot say with me, "I believe in miracles"?

6

Bruce Baker
Take God at His Word

Two more grateful people you will never meet. Often standing on the platform, I look down into the faces of the folk standing in the crowd, and I see Mr. and Mrs. Bruce Baker. Our eyes meet, and we nod our greeting; our hearts blend as one in gratitude and thanksgiving to the Lord for God's mercy in healing Bruce.

Bruce Baker worked for a large bottling company in Youngstown, Ohio. It was in the early fall of 1948 when his illness began.

It all started with what seemed to be an innocent-enough, hacking cough. Bruce wasn't in the least worried. He figured that cutting down on his smoking and a box of cough drops would fix him up. It didn't—the cough grew worse until he began to take a bottle of cough syrup with him to work every day, dosing himself at regular

47

intervals. But the coughing spells became increasingly frequent and severe.

One night in October he came home from work feeling miserably ill. Feverish, his chest sore from continuous coughing, he said to his wife, "Guess I have bronchitis, Geneva." He doctored at home for a few days, and then returned to work, feeling a bit better, but still far from well.

Three weeks later, on November 2, he came home from work one day at noon—too sick to stand on his feet. He was not to work again for almost five years.

That first night of his illness was to set a pattern for the many nights to come over the next eight months.

He went to bed with a high fever: at 7:00 P.M. he suffered a violent chill. In spite of the hot water bottle and extra blankets his wife piled upon him, he continued in its grip until after four o'clock the next morning. That afternoon the doctor diagnosed his illness as viral pneumonia. For thirty days he was treated for this disease, and his condition continued to grow worse rather than to improve.

Each afternoon Bruce watched fearfully as the hands of the clock crept toward six o'clock. He had learned to dread that hour, for he knew only too well what lay in store for him. With devastating regularity the same pattern repeated itself night after night. Between six and seven o'clock, he would be seized with a hard chill, so violent that the entire bed would shake and the chattering of his teeth could be heard in the next room. From the hour that the chilling began, he would alternately chill and sweat and chill and sweat throughout the night until five or so in the morning when he would fall into an exhausted sleep, lasting for perhaps an hour when he would be awakened again by a coughing spell.

Whether the chill, or the sweating, or the coughing were more distressing would be difficult to say, for when the chill broke, his body would be bathed in perspiration and his bed soaked clear through to the mattress. His wife Geneva had to change his bed at least four times a night, and so weakening were these heavy sweats, that the doctor expressed grave concern.

But now the most frightening symptom of all evidenced itself: each time that he would cough in the grip of a chill, he would find himself unable to breathe, and no medication seemed to relieve this terrifying shortage of breath.

"Many a time," relates his wife, "his face would turn black, and his tongue would be hanging out of his mouth, as he tried to physically force the air in and out of his lungs."

And many was the night that Geneva spent in prayer, sitting and kneeling by his bedside the whole night through. "I knew that God was his only salvation," she says simply.

At the end of thirty days, prostrate from the alternate chills and sweating, exhausted by continual coughing; suffering from an increasing difficulty breathing, Bruce was in serious condition. The doctor knew that viral pneumonia was not sufficient to explain his illness.

During the next few months, in an effort to get at the source of his illness, Bruce was tested for malaria, psitticosis (parrot fever), tuberculosis and undulant fever. All these tests proved negative, and his illness continued unabated.

Finally one of the doctors at the South Side Hospital in

Youngstown, Ohio, questioned him closely about the nature of his work before he was stricken ill. The physician discovered that an alkali was mixed with water in the bottle washer for sterilization purposes. Bruce worked outside using a stick to stir the mixture, but the doctor's theory was that when the wind would blow, Bruce must have inhaled large quantities of the fumes. The physician suspected lung damage from this cause and suggested that the patient be taken to Blogden Clinic in Cleveland to have this tentative diagnosis confirmed. This was done and the clinic found that his lungs had indeed been badly burned from the inhalation of alkali fumes at the plant. His illness was diagnosed as emphysema and bronchial asthma. He underwent a lengthy course of treatment in Cleveland, but his condition did not improve.

Although many people have never heard of emphysema, it is more prevalent than lung cancer and tuberculosis combined. It is difficult to diagnose, and is often mistaken for bronchitis or broncial asthma.

In this disease the lungs fill up with air that the patient cannot exhale (his difficulty in breathing lies in the fact that he cannot breathe *out*). Eventually the over-extended lungs lose their elasticity. The diaphragm, which moves freely up and down during the normal breathing process, gradually flattens and becomes immobile. The normal person at rest breathes about 14 times a minute, while the victim of emphysema breathes up to 30 times a minute and still cannot get enough oxygen. He suffers from a chronic and generalized oxygen deficiency, and his muscles weaken from lack of oxygen and disuse, until the least activity involves almost superhuman effort on the part of the patient.

Another characteristic of the disease is the patient's inability, no matter how hard he coughs, to expel the mucus which troubles him. As he strains futilely to cough it up, the bronchial passageways rupture. Swollen and scarred, they thicken and become increasingly narrow. There is no known medical cure for this condition— only attempted palliative treatment, which in some cases helps and in others does not. All its victims, regardless of treatment, are doomed to live out their lives fighting a battle of breathlessness.

The extent of incapacitation depends on the damage done to the lungs. In Bruce's case, his lungs were badly burned and, according to medical opinion, severely and permanently damaged. His incapacitation was virtually total.

For eight months after the first misdiagnosis of viral pneumonia, Bruce continued to suffer the night-long chills. Not more than three times during this period did he go more than two consecutive nights without them. When finally permitted out of bed for short periods of time, he found himself unable to take more than a few steps without suffering acute distress from lack of breath.

"Our bedroom was next to the kitchen," he relates, "but when I walked from there into the kitchen for a meal, I would collapse at the table and have to sit there for fifteen minutes before I could eat a bite."

The months extended into years, during which Bruce was hospitalized three times in Youngstown, and under the care of a total of nine doctors. No one and no treatment could help him. For over four years he could not work—all he could do was, as he puts it, "sit or lie."

On a few memorable summer days during these years, however, he was able to walk slowly, pausing to struggle for breath, into the yard.

"There he would sit," recalls Geneva, "and watch me mow the lawn, and tears would stream down his face that I had to do it while he sat helplessly by."

Bruce was not then a Christian but as he says, "I did *know* that God could do *anything.*"

Bruce and his wife had listened to the broadcasts, and three or four times during this period of Bruce's illness, Geneva had taken him to the services.

"I'll never know how I ever managed to get there let alone stand in line all that time waiting for the doors to open," says Bruce. "This fact in itself proves how much God has been with us all along.

"The very first time we went, and I saw people healed by God, I knew better than ever how wonderful He was. I knew that afternoon that I was a sinner, but I also knew that God loved me, and what He had done for others He would do for me. When I saw how my wife so frequently prayed for me all night, often not going to bed at all," Bruce continued, "I realized that if I were to be healed it would take my prayer, too. I wasn't very good at praying, but I did the best I knew how."

It was noon on an early November Tuesday in 1952, when Geneva said to her husband, "I wish you would write a prayer request to Miss Kuhlman. But *you* do it, not I—because this thing is between you and the Lord."

While he was sitting at the kitchen table, she brought him a pencil and paper. He wrote the request at once, and Geneva went right out and mailed it.

The next Saturday—four days later—Geneva had

planned to work for a few hours for her sister in Masury, Ohio, where she had a store and a restaurant. With Bruce out of work for four years almost to the day, and no money coming in except at the last a few dollars from the workmen's compensation fund, the Bakers were having a hard time getting along, and Geneva was glad to earn any money she could, without having to leave her sick husband for too long a time.

She was very nervous about leaving him on this particular Saturday. He seemed, if anything, worse than usual, and if anything were to happen to him, he couldn't reach her by phone. They had long since had the telephone taken out because they couldn't afford it.

She was so worried that she toyed with the idea of not going to Masury, but they decided that she would simply have to risk it: they needed every cent she could earn to pay for four tons of coal which had been delivered the day before, and lay now out in the yard, waiting till Sunday when a good friend had promised to come and shovel it into their cellar for them.

Geneva had been gone for half an hour, and Bruce was sitting in his accustomed chair.

"All at once," he says, "I just seemed to know that this was the time to take God at His Word—'by my stripes you are healed'—so I just looked up and asked God to heal me as I had seen Him heal so many others."

Immediately Bruce felt a great, spreading warmth in his chest, and then he became deathly sick. He was badly frightened at the way he felt, and then, he relates, he said to himself, "Don't be afraid of God. This is what you have asked for."

He staggered into his bathroom and leaned on the basin

for support while he got his breath. And suddenly there came from his mouth what he describes as "The equivalent of a large water glass full of heavy, clear fluid." When he raised his head, *he took his first deep breath in four years.*

"It felt too wonderful to even try to describe," he smiles in recollection. "I went into the yard, and walked up and down, up and down, without stopping—laughing and crying and thanking God all at the same time."

When Geneva got back from her sister's that evening, she noticed that the pile of coal was almost gone from the back yard. Bruce had shoveled three of the four tons of coal. As she went into the house, she called first, "Are you all right, honey?"

At his quick, affirmative response, she asked, on her way to the bedroom, "Who was nice enough to throw our coal into the cellar while I was gone?"

"I did," came the reply.

Bruce walked out then into the living room, to greet his wife. She took one look at his face, and knew what had happened. Together on their knees, they thanked God.

That night at dinner, Geneva asked her husband, "Honey, how come you left that tiny little pile of coal still out in the yard? Did you get awfully tired before you got it all in?"

"No," Bruce replied with a grin, "But Noble has made his plans to come over tomorrow and get the coal in for us, and I didn't want him to get here and not find any so I left that little pile for him!"

Two days later, Bruce Baker, who for more than four years had not been able to take five steps without inducing a severe coughing spell and without having to stop and gasp for breath, walked the entire two miles from his house to town. He paused in front of the courthouse and looked up—four stories high and, as he well knew, there were elevators but he chose to walk. He took a deep breath, walked briskly into the building, and hardly slackening his pace, walked up the four flights of stairs and down again! *This is* God.

Bruce Baker was healed ten years ago. Doctors can find nothing wrong with him, and attest to the fact that his lungs are perfect.

He has gone into gardening work now, for a living, and among other things, he follows the power lawnmower up and down slopes, from eight o'clock in the morning until often after three o'clock in the afternoon. "You don't do *that* if you don't have good lungs," Bruce smiles.

And then he goes on to say, radiating joy as he speaks, "There are just no words to say how one feels when God heals us. Geneva and I thank Him every day of our lives, and try to do something for Him in return."

Active faith believes God to the point of action. "I just seemed to know that this was the time to *take God at His Word*."

I have always been thrilled to that glorious account of Joshua and the children of Israel taking that last march around the walls of Jericho. The Lord had promised them the city. The seventh day came, and six times they had marched around the wall of the city, not a brick had moved, not an inch of mortar out of place, and not even a crack in the wall, *But God had promised!*

"And it came to pass at the seventh time, when the priests blew with the trumpets, Joshua said unto the people, Shout; for the Lord hath given you the city" (Josh. 6:16).

Not the tiniest break in the wall, and not a brick had fallen! "And the people shouted with a great shout, that the wall fell down *flat,* so that the people went up into the city, every man straight before him, and they took the city."

The secret of victory was this shout of faith which dared to claim a promised victory on the authority of God's Word alone! It is when active faith dares to believe God to the point of action, that something has to happen.

7

Betty Fox
"That's God!"

I shall never forget the first time I saw her—a cute little girl, if I ever saw one—about five feet two, with brown eyes framed by long, dark lashes. I could easily understand why they used to call her "Betty Boop" in the restaurant where she worked in Rochester, Pennsylvania.

It was hard for me to believe that this "girl" was not a girl at all, but the mother of a grown son. It would doubtless be even harder for those not familiar with the power of God to believe that not long before, this vivacious, radiantly healthy woman had been in the last stages of multiple sclerosis.

Betty Fox had been ill for years with this merciless disease for which there is as yet no known medical cure; a disease which in spite of palliative treatment and falsely encouraging temporary remissions, follows a relentless course of progressive crippling until the patient finally becomes helpless.

Betty had reached this point by the spring of 1950. She hadn't been out of her fourth-floor, walk-up apartment for months, except when her husband carried her to the doctor—for by this time she was completely unable to walk.

When her husband was home, he took care of her and carried her around like a baby. When he wasn't there to carry her, she crawled on the floor to wherever she had to get, but even by this method she couldn't get far, impeded as she was by her now virtually useless arms.

Of course some days were better than others—a characteristic of the disease—and on her "good" days, she got along slightly better; which is to say, that on these days she was able to tortuously maneuver herself from chair leg to chair leg, and thus could cover a greater distance.

Her legs were ice cold and numb, and so were her arms up to the elbows. Her hands were useless, unable to pick up or grasp anything. For a long time she had to be fed—a task which kindly neighbors took turns in performing for her each midday, when her husband was at work.

"And when they tried to feed me," recalls Betty, "I would often shake so badly that they couldn't get the spoon to my mouth."

Betty's prognosis at this time was very poor. In addition to multiple sclerosis, her heart was threatened. The doctor had told her husband and son that it could not indefinitely survive the severe punishment it was taking from the constant, palsy-like trembling induced by her disease.

It was one day in April that her son, who worked at

Kroger's market, said "Mother—why don't you go to those services on the North Side where Kathryn Kuhlman is preaching? When I pass by Carnegie Auditorium on the way to and from work, I see people *walking* out to the ambulances in which they were brought to the services. I've seen people walking carrying their crutches. Why don't you go and see what happens?"

Betty replied quickly, "Well, honey, I'm just too far gone. The doctors all say there's absolutely nothing to be done."

"Listen, mom," her son said firmly, "I've seen them go in on stretchers and I've seen them walk out. If this can happen to others, it can happen to you."

The boy kept urging his mother, until at last she agreed to at least listen to the daily broadcasts, but this was easier said than done for she was totally unable to grasp the knob to turn the radio on.

Each day before leaving for work, her husband would seat her either on the davenport or in a comfortable chair, with the radio beside her. But there she was forced to remain—helpless—until someone would come along to assist her.

It was a Friday morning in early May that a friend stopped in a few minutes before the broadcast was due to begin.

"Betty," she said, "I wrote in a prayer request for you, and I want you to listen to it today."

She turned the radio on for Betty, and they sat together on the sofa, listening, but Betty's name was not mentioned over the air.

The next day, Saturday, when there was no broadcast, another friend happened in to see Betty. They were sitting in the living room talking together, when suddenly it happened—

"I thought it was just another of the regular shaking spells," relates Betty, "and then I began to shake so hard, I knew this was something entirely different. My friend was so badly frightened that she went home. She told me later that she thought I was dying. I was scared and began to crawl through the hall and then I met my sister-in-law who was just coming in to visit me, and she took me into the living room.

"I was sitting there," Betty continues, "shaking so hard by now I thought I would fall apart, but this shaking was different! My sister-in-law thought maybe a cigarette would help me—so she lit one and handed it to me, but I just couldn't smoke it. Then suddenly, and instantly, as if someone had turned off an electric switch, I stopped shaking."

Betty's little three-year-old nephew was in the room at the time, and he said, "What happened, Aunt Betty, that all of a sudden you stopped shaking like that?" As he asked the question, she knew the answer—"I—I think God healed me," she replied, and she was right.

At that moment Betty had received her healing. From that moment on, she was never again to suffer that palsy-like shaking. Her arms had instantaneously lost their numbness, as had her legs, and she immediately regained the full use of her hands. With no effort whatsoever, she leaned over and turned off the radio, and picked up a book she had accidentally knocked to the floor in her excitement.

In one respect alone, her healing was not instantaneous. "I had to learn to walk all over again," she says, "and like a child, I had to learn to go up and down steps, but this took only a very little while."

Betty was so excited at what had happened, that she called in everyone in the apartment house to see—and when in a few days she was walking everywhere, the people in her apartment who had never seen her walk before, watched her in speechless amazement.

The local doctor who had examined her just four weeks prior to her healing was aghast when she *walked* into his office late one afternoon—her coordination perfect—and apparently able to do anything and everything with her body, for she announced to him that that day she had cleaned her house, washed and ironed, and spent two hours working out in the yard!

He thoroughly examined her, could find no trace of either the multiple sclerosis or the heart condition, and then, reports Betty, "He made me walk back and forth on the main street of Rochester in front of his office.

"He watched me with such a funny expression on his face, and then he said to me—as he has a great many times since—'you certainly are lucky, and you should be so thankful. If you had lived at all, I should never have expected to see you out of a wheelchair. None of us had anything to do with this. It must have been God.'"

Betty knew this full well, and in deep gratitude to God, she accepted Jesus as her Saviour, giving Him her heart and her life, to use in His service.

She hadn't been inside a church since she could remember, and had smoked heavily for twenty-two years. Immediately after her healing, she completely changed her way of life. One of the first things she did was to give up smoking, for as she says: "Nobody knows until you haven't had the use of your body for a long time, what it is like to be normal and healthy again. And when you know it is God himself who has healed you, you just can't praise Him enough or do enough for Him."

Nearly everyone in Rochester knows Betty, as she worked so long there in a popular restaurant—where she recalls, somewhat to her embarrassment, how most of the regular patrons called her "Betty Boop." Through her witness, many of these same people have been brought to Christ.

Before her healing, Betty and her husband had not attended any church. Now they began to go every Sunday morning to the First Methodist Church in Rochester. Knowing well the power of prayer, they were delighted to find that the minister of this church prayed regularly for the sick—kneeling himself at the altar and inviting any members of the congregation who so wished, to go to the altar rail and pray in silence for spiritual or physical healing.

After the Foxes had been attending this church for some weeks, the minister came out to see them about joining the church.

As Betty says: "My husband testifies as enthusiastically as I do about my healing, and he could hardly wait to tell the Rev. Stump all about it."

Rev. Stump, a firm believer in faith healing, was greatly interested. The following Sunday he inserted a questionnaire in the Church bulletin, which was passed out at the service, with the request that it be marked and placed in the collection plate.

In this questionnaire the pastor reiterated his personal faith in prayer and divine healing. Emphasizing that the way in which his church prayed for the sick was only one means of attempting to carry out the command of Jesus to preach, to teach and to heal, he asked his congregation to express their views concerning (A) the method of prayer then being used, and (B) whether they wished such prayers continued as part of the regular church service. The overwhelming majority of the congregation of four hundred voted to continue the prayers.

Betty had had wonderful parents, and she had received a good Christian upbringing in her youth. Although she had wandered far from their influence, she had always known in her heart that God could heal. She knew this when her son had first mentioned the services at Carnegie Auditorium.

"But I didn't think He would heal *me,* because I didn't think I was good enough, and I knew I hadn't lived right. But I was wrong. God in His mercy *did* heal me."

Had Betty known more about God before she was healed, she would never have made the initial mistake of thinking that He would refuse to heal her because she "was not good enough."

Have *you* ever wondered what God is really like? The only perfect revelation God ever made of himself, he made in Jesus Christ, and if you will look at Him through Jesus Christ, you will know what kind of a God He is really like, for Jesus said: "He that hath seen Me hath seen the Father" (John 14:9).

Did you hear Him speak to blind Bartimaeus, the beggar? The crowd took no notice whatsoever of the beggar in their midst, till he began to cry: "Jesus, Thou son of David, have mercy on me." The disciples said: "Shut up, you beggar," but Jesus said tenderly: "Bartimaeus, recieve thy sight." THAT'S GOD!

Did you see Him moved with compassion for the restless, hungry multitude who were like sheep without a shepherd? Jesus said, "I have compassion on the multitude, because they continue with me now for three days, and have nothing to eat: I will not send them away fasting, lest they faint on the way." THAT'S GOD!

Did you see Him weeping in pity over Jerusalem? You have had an idea that God is a vindictive God and that He delights in letting a man go to Hell: but you do not know God if you think that. See his great heart of mercy overflowing with tenderness and compassion as he cries: "How often would I have gathered thy children together, even as a hen gathered her chickens under her wing, and ye would not." THAT'S GOD!

Did you hear him speak to the poor woman with the scarlet stain of sin on her soul—the woman who was taken in the very act of adultery—the harlot being dragged into His presence by her accusers? The crowd wanted to stone her, but Jesus said: "Go in peace and sin no more." THAT'S GOD!

If you want a single word to characterize the person of God, all you will have to do is to take four letters and write them over and over again from the beginning to the end—the word, LOVE—AND THAT'S GOD!

Did you see the precious young woman—her frail little body racked with pain from the pitiless disease of multiple sclerosis—a woman who had not been to church in years, who had never really served God a day of her life; so ignorant regarding spiritual things that when the power of God came upon her body, a sister-in-law, wanting to be helpful, lit a cigarette and put it in the suffering woman's mouth, thinking it would stop the "shaking"? In tender mercy, and out of His great compassion, the Master touched that body and made it whole. My friend, THAT'S GOD!

A God who understands; a God who knows our every weakness, our every failure, our every shortcoming, our every sin—and yet He continues to love us and to pour his mercy upon us. He loves us, not because we are weak; not because of our failures; not because of our sins; but because we are His children. And He loves each one of us as though we were His only child.

In that moment, God honored the simple faith, the simple confidence of Betty Fox, who dared to stretch forth a helpless hand to touch the One who has all power in heaven and earth. As her faith met God, something happened: something *always* happens when simple faith meets God.

When the power of God went through the body of Betty Fox, she was so lacking in spiritual knowledge that she did not have the slightest idea that it was the supernatural power of God flowing through her body. She had never attended a service; she had never seen anyone healed by the power of God; she had never in her life witnessed a miracle, nor had she ever seen me. She had seen Him, and that was sufficient!

Several weeks ago, exactly ten years and seven months after her healing, Betty returned to one of her former doctors. He found her in perfect health, with no signs of multiple sclerosis.

It was as if he were thinking out loud when he said to her: "No mere remission of multiple sclerosis ever lasted this long, and there is no indication whatsoever that you have ever suffered from that disease. The good Lord has

taken care of you when we could not."
THAT'S GOD!

8

The Erskines
"Heal My Wife, Jesus"

The telegram read: "Please pray that it won't rain tomorrow!"

I laughed out loud. The telegrams usually say: "Please pray for the healing of cancer or please pray for the healing of something else." But this!

The wire had come on Saturday, and the next day was the Sunday Service at Butler. Apparently I was supposed to touch the throne of God and ask God to hold back the rain clouds so that it wouldn't rain on the day of the service! Feeling very much on the spot, all I could do was look up and say, "Heavenly Father, you know all about this. Whatever is involved, please take care of everything."

This is the story of the marvelous way in which God *did* take care of everything for the Erskine family.

I was to find out later who had sent that telegram and why.

"I was desperate," said Louise, the young married daughter of James and Edith Erskine. "Mother was in the hospital dying of cancer. The hospital authorities had told dad and me six weeks before I sent the wire that we could take mother out of the hospital for a few hours— just long enough to bring her to one of your services in Butler—but *only* if the weather was good. If it were raining, the danger of her catching cold would be too great a risk.

"It rained for five Sundays in a row," Louise went on, "So we couldn't bring her. Meanwhile mother was getting worse and worse and we knew it would soon be too late. So after visiting her that Saturday afternoon, I stopped at a telegraph office and sent you that telegram."

Louise and her father had moved heaven and earth to procure permission from the hospital at Tarentum to release Mrs. Erskine long enough to attend that service. Theirs had been an unorthodox request to say the least, and it was only through the influence of Dr. Cross, who had seen others of his patients miraculously cured by the power of God, that permission was finally granted.

For five successive Saturday nights, Louise had driven in to the hospital to fix her mother's hair and get her all ready for the service next day, and for five successive Sunday mornings James Erskine had arisen at dawn and gone to Butler, to stand in line for many hours waiting for the doors of the auditorium to open so as to be sure to have a seat ready for his wife when Louise brought her in from the hospital. And on each of these five Sundays it had started to rain an hour before the service was to begin.

Hence you can understand the situation which prompted the sending of that telegram!

When Louise and Mr. Erskine arose that last Sunday morning, the first thing they did was to peer anxiously out the window. A clear and cloudless sky greeted their gaze. They were overjoyed—obviously the prayer for a good day had been answered. As James took off for Butler, and Louise left her home in Bakerstown to pick up her mother at the hospital, their hearts were filled with thanksgiving to God. At last Edith was going to make that service!

Louise brought her in that day from the hospital as planned and Mr. Erskine took her back after the service. He had just carried her safely inside the hospital doors, when a downpour of rain began.

It had been early in the spring of 1951 when father and daughter learned that Edith had cancer of the liver.

As Dr. Cross had expressed it: "Her liver is like your grandmother's old lace curtain. But whatever you do," warned the doctor, "don't tell her she has cancer or she'll give up immediately. Actually, however, there is nothing we can do except give her enough drugs to relieve her pain. She may linger or she may go quickly. There is no way to tell." Her weight at this time was seventy pounds, down from 168.

Some weeks before Edith was hospitalized, she and Louise had begun to attend the services at Carnegie Hall.

"It was there," says Louise, "That Miss Kuhlman taught me the value of fasting, explaining that it was an expression of the fervor of one's prayers. I remember one service in particular where she used David as an example. She explained how he had coupled his prayers with humiliation and self-denial, and that therein lay their power: and how he was so intent in his devotion and desire that he had no appetite.

"Now that mother was so desperately ill," Louise continued, "All that Miss Kuhlman had ever said about fasting came back to me. Mother just *couldn't* die. I had three younger sisters who needed their mother desperately—three little girls who needed their mother's teaching, who needed her love, and a home. If ever there was a time for fasting, this was it."

From the time it was established that her mother had cancer, Louise could be found every Friday afternoon at the Miracle Service—fasting from sunup to sundown. It was not of herself she was thinking when she pleaded before the throne of God for her mother's recovery, but of the three little sisters at home. She was touched and moved when she learned that they, too, unknown to her, were going without food all day every Friday.

"And I shall never forget as long as I live," said Louise, "the first morning when I went to pack daddy's lunch pail and he asked that no food be placed in his bucket—just water. Nobody knows what that means to a miner. Only a man who has worked in the mines knows what it is like to work underground for hours without food."

For five long days James Erskine was to go into the Ford Collyer Coal Mines with only water in his lunch bucket, but never once did he ever think of it in the light of a sacrifice. Never once did he ever say he was hungry. Never once did there issue from his lips a word of complaint. He was BELIEVING GOD for the healing of his wife. He was believing a God who could not lie.

These were rough days for James. He was completely on his own with the three small children at home. He cooked and cleaned and washed and ironed their clothes. He would come home directly from work to check on them, then go to the hospital, then go back home to get their supper; and then back to the hospital where he usually stayed until midnight and sometimes the whole night through.

"Often," his wife says, "I would open my eyes and find him on his knees by my bed."

To see him thus made Edith, sick as she was, rejoice and praise God—for to see James like this was an entirely new and wonderful experience.

Little had the Erskines known in the beginning how wonderfully God was to lead them, as a family, step by step, preparing them and waiting for them to prepare *themselves* for the miracle which was to be wrought for Edith.

"Daddy had always been a good father," said Louise, "but far from a religious man. He never went to church, and I as his daughter could never remember seeing him open a Bible."

To be sure, James Erskine had had religious training as a young lad, for his father had been a devout Christian who had believed implicitly in divine healing. But although as a young boy he had been brought up in the full faith, he had long since lost interest in all religious things.

Mr. Erskine had often wondered when his daughter went to the services at Carnegie Hall, what on earth could be enthralling enough to warrant anyone *standing* for five hours, as when unable to procure a seat, she frequently did.

One day his curiosity got the better of him and he resolved to see for himself. In a casual, offhanded manner, he volunteered to go with her.

71

They set off together for the auditorium, but as they arrived at the doors, James had a change of heart. He adamantly refused to go inside the building. "I just didn't want to get that close to anything religious," he says now in smiling recollection.

Irritated with himself for having made the trip, he contemplated returning home, but then he decided he might as well wait it out for Louise; so as the service began, he sat down outside on the auditorium steps.

"I couldn't see Miss Kuhlman, of course," he says, "but I could hear her voice from where I sat, and suddenly I heard her say, 'The method by which God transforms a life is found in Ephesians 2:5-6: *Even when we were dead in sins, God hath quickened us together with Christ (by grace we are saved) and hath raised us up together.* To quicken means to give life. If we are dead, we need life, and that is what is given when a man accepts Christ as his Saviour. God does not patch up the old life, or make certain repairs on the old life; He gives a new life, through the new birth.

" 'God supplies the MIRACLE of the new birth experience—He supplies the power—Jesus supplies the pardon, but we must supply the *willingness!* God cannot help a man unless he is willing to give himself completely to Him: wanting to be delivered from sin, more than anything else in the whole world. Any man who will be dead honest in praying this simple prayer: *I believe Thou art the Son of the Eternal God, and I accept Thee as my Saviour,* will not only be pardoned by Him, but will be delivered from the power of sin and will be *quickened* by the Holy Spirit of God.'

"Why, I had heard my father say the same thing time

and time again," says James. "It was a queer sensation. I felt as if I were a little boy again, listening to my father talk to me about the things of God."

The influence of a godly parent is never lost. Sitting there on the steps of Carnegie Hall, listening to a disembodied voice, which in a curious way became for him the voice of his father, James Erskine relived his youth. And he relived the death of his father many years before.

The great West Virginia mine disaster occurred in 1927. When the Everettsville Mine of the New England Fuel and Transportation Company was wrecked by a tremendous explosion on April 30 of that year, it was at first supposed that all the men trapped inside had been instantly killed. However, this theory was dispelled with the finding of the last three bodies, one of whom was James's father.

In a dinner pail was found scrawled messages written to one of the trapped miners' wives. These messages were written on one slip of paper, perhaps the only paper he could find down in the mine. He wrote as life was slowly leaving their bodies; the words came from the heart and mind of a dying man:

> April 20—Time 6:20. Dear wife—still alive but the air is very bad—oh, how I love you Mary—dear father, I will be going soon. We are just cold and when the air comes it will be bad as we are on the return side. Will meet you all in heaven. We have plenty of time to make peace with the Lord. Signed, H. Russell.
>
> Will soon be going to leave this world. Stay in America and give kids a home. Marry again if

you take a notion, but God bless you and the kids. Signed, H. Russell.

At peace with God, and dear Mary, tell father I was saved. Also the Erskines. We do not feel any pain. Try and stay in West Virginia. Love to the kids. Signed: Russell.

We are going to Heaven. We have plenty of time to make peace with the Lord. Signed, H. R.

We are weakening—our hearts are beating fast—goodby everybody. Signed, H. R.

We don't feel bad—all we think about is our families.

H.R.

A thousand memories rushed through the mind of James Erskine as he sat on the steps of Carnegie Hall, and he knew better than anyone else in the whole world that *he* was not ready to meet his God!

Sitting on those auditorium steps, James remembered with poignant vividness, the hours his father had spent telling him of the love and mercy of God. He remembered his father saying to him: "Live by God, son, and you will know all your life the *peace that passeth all understanding.*"

And most of all he remembered the prayers that his father had prayed, that his son would experience salvation.

In that very hour of teeming memories, touched off by a voice repeating almost forgotten and largely discarded scriptural truths, something happened to James. In that hour his father's prayers—perhaps the very prayers uttered in that mine before death came—were answered.

Years had come and gone, but God never turns a deaf ear to the prayers of a sincere man. Much water had gone over the dam, but God never forgets, and on this afternoon, twenty-four years later, He answered the prayers of a God-fearing man that his son might be saved. "When I heard you that day," says James, "I all at once got hungry for God. I had quit going to church eighteen years before, but now I wanted to go back. In those years I'd done a lot of drinking—day and night—and while I always managed to support my family, I spent an awful lot on liquor, sometimes as much as forty dollars over a weekend. The drinking and all my other sins crowded in, and suddenly I wanted more than anything else to get rid of them all. Right then and there, I bowed my head and asked God to forgive me. Sitting on those steps, I gave my heart and my life to Christ."

That night, going home from the service, Louise waited anxiously for some expression from her father: perhaps curses because he had had to wait; perhaps a rebuke because the service was so long. But not one word did he speak.

After they arrived home he turned, and with all the earnestness and sincerity of one whose life had been transformed by the power of God, he said: "It was just as though I heard my father speak again tonight. Everything Miss Kuhlman said was exactly what I was taught by him. I have asked God to forgive my sins, and I have accepted Jesus as my Saviour."

A week later, with tears of joy streaming down her face, Louise was to say: "We have a new dad. I come home now and instead of seeing him with a glass of liquor in his hand, I find him reading the Bible."

There was no bargaining here on the part of James. He had not said; "Heal my wife, Jesus, and I will believe." He believed *first*. His soul was saved while his wife lay dying, for to the best of his knowledge she had not been healed at the Butler service.

James's salvation was the first miracle to occur in the Erskine family: the second was soon to follow.

"On Wednesday night," relates Louise, "Daddy had taken a little radio to the hospital so that mother could hear Miss Kuhlman's broadcast the next morning, feeling that it would do much to strengthen her faith and give her the hope she needed."

As Mr. Erskine left the hospital that night, he only *hoped* that Edith could get the broadcast the next day. The poor little old radio was so antiquated and powerless, that most of the time all it would do was crackle and pop, but he had left it in Edith's hospital room just in case. Perhaps it, too, would experience a conversion!

"Miss Kuhlman didn't have the slightest idea what was going on," says Louise, "We had sent in a prayer request for mother several days before, and lo and behold, on that Thursday morning she read it over the air and prayed for 'the Mrs. Erskine dying of cancer in Tarentum Hospital.'"

Louise, listening at home in Bakerstown, was terrified that her mother might have heard her name over the air and thus for the first time found out the nature of her disease. She rushed over to the hospital, fearful of the emotional state in which she might find Edith.

Sure enough, for the first time, the little radio had played without crackling, and the broadcast had come over as clear as a bell. Her mother had heard every word.

When Louise walked in, the sick woman said, "I heard the broadcast, and I know about the woman dying of cancer of the liver," and then she began to cry, and said, "I'm not afraid to die; just don't let the children at home ever be separated. That's all that worries me." She closed her eyes then, and said nothing more.

Next day at broadcast time, Louise was with her mother, kneeling beside the bed as they listened together— "I heard Miss Kuhlman say, 'I feel impelled to pray again for the woman at Tarentum Hospital dying of cancer of the liver.' "

And suddenly it happened.

"In the middle of the prayer," reports Louise, "the power went through mother, and I couldn't hold her in bed, so violently was she shaking and crying. A nurse came running in, and they began giving her hypodermics. They didn't know what was wrong with her, but of course I knew what was happening. She was under the power.

From that moment on, Edith began to pick up. The pain left; she began to eat ravenously, and immediately began to gain weight—as much as three pounds a day. The doctors, frankly incredulous at this weight gain recorded by the nurses, proceeded to weigh her themselves each day.

She was out of the hospital, hale and hearty, within a matter of days.

When she was first hospitalized, before her condition had become so desperately critical, Dr. Cross had suggested to the family the possibility of taking her to the Lahey Clinic in Boston. If they deemed it advisable there, surgery might be performed in the hope of prolonging her life. These arrangements had been made, but when Edith's condition became so acute, the trip to Boston, and possible surgery, were obviously out of the question.

However, now it was a different story. Mrs. Erskine *appeared* to be healed. As Dr. Cross was to say: "There certainly must be something to your preacher lady." But medically speaking, such a healing was impossible. In the event, then, that her apparent recovery was merely a spectacular remission of the disease, Dr. Cross urged her to go to Boston to the clinic. He pointed out that the doctors there were already familiar with her case, and after examining her, might think it advisable to operate, notwithstanding what appeared to be her cure.

At first she and her family demurred. They *knew* she had been healed by the power of God—and furthermore, what about the expense involved? They estimated that it would cost in the neighborhood of $3,000 to have this operation performed, which they were convinced wasn't necessary.

And then it developed that the Miners' Welfare would finance the operation. Edith finally agreed, saying: "All right. If they want to pay $3,000 to find out that I don't have cancer, let them go ahead! At least this will prove to anyone who has ever doubted, that God performs miracles of healing."

Her husband took her to Boston and stayed the entire time, losing nineteen working days. Due to the extraordinary circumstances of the case, Dr. Lahey himself operated. No trace of cancer anywhere in this woman's body was found—only *scar tissue* indicating that surgery had *already* been done. It had—by the Great Physician himself, who had preceded Dr. Lahey.

Edith Erskine's healing took place eleven years ago. She is today in perfect health, weighing 168 pounds. She does all her own housework, and frequently helps her neighbors do their wall washing and other heavy cleaning.

This is a miracle of God, but an even greater miracle is the wonderful change that came over the life of the man who was once so far from God, and who, sitting on the steps of Carnegie Hall, was so instantly transformed by His power.

A short while ago the Erskines moved to Southern California, where James has taken a new job. They left their Pittsburgh home for only one purpose; to be near their unsaved son in California—to exert upon him their Christian influence, that he, too, might be brought to Christ.

God never inflicts disease, but He permitted and used Edith's cancer that it might bring the whole Erskine family to Him.

I still contend that the greatest miracle in the world is the transformation of a life. Mrs. Erskine's healing of cancer was indeed a miracle, but the greater of the two was the spiritual healing which took place in the life of her husband.

> I'll trust in God's unchanging Word,
> till soul and body sever:
> For though all else shall pass away,
> His Word shall stand forever.

> —MARTIN LUTHER

9

Mrs. Fischer's Baby
The Power of Prayer

The service was never scheduled to begin before seven o'clock in the evening. But every afternoon on the dot of four, there could be seen a little girl of about twelve years of age, standing amidst the great crowd outside of Carnegie Auditorium. Like the hundreds of others among whom she stood, this child was waiting for the moment when the doors would be opened, and at the moment of their opening, she would invariably rush frantically for a seat. There she would remain for three hours, never leaving her seat for a single moment, her only movement an occasional turning of the head to watch the doors of the hall.

At seven o'clock sharp, a woman would come in carrying a baby—its head always carefully covered, but the covering could not entirely conceal its hideous deformity:

the tiny child was suffering from the tragic affliction of hydrocephalus (water on the brain).

As soon as she saw this woman and baby enter the doors, the twelve-year-old girl would stand up and wave. The woman, seeing the small beckoning hand of her young daughter, would wend her way through the standing crowd to the aisle in which she sat. The youngster would then relinquish her long-held seat to her mother and baby sister. She herself would remain on her feet during the entire three hours of the service.

It wasn't until months later that I found out that the twelve-year-old child, Helen Fischer, was the oldest daughter of a family of seven girls. Helen would come directly from school to the auditorium, without having a bite to eat, while her mother was at home getting supper ready for the rest of the family.

Helen knew that her mother would never get a seat at the service with the vast crowd always in attendance, were she to wait until after dinner to come; and it was out of the question for her mother to stand for all those hours with a heavy baby in her arms. Helen thus cooperated by coming hours before in order to assure her mother a seat.

Actually this was considerably more than mere cooperation on her part. It was in a very real sense, an offering of herself made in Jesus' Name, for the healing of her baby sister.

To this very day, I sincerely believe that this young girl was the key to the remarkable healing which was to follow.

The Fischers already had six children when Baby Billie came along, but each one had been wanted, and the birth of each had been a cause for as much rejoicing as if it had been the first. Baby Billie was no exception; the seventh child, perhaps, and also the seventh daughter, but there was as much joy at her coming as there had been when Helen was born twelve years before.

It soon became obvious, however, that something was dreadfully wrong with the new baby, and only a mother can know the mother Fischer's agony when she was told that her new baby was a victim of congenital hydrocephalus.

Helen would offer the baby a rattle, but no small hands reached out to grasp it. She would dangle a bright colored toy in front of the infant, but there was no reaction. She would enter or leave a room, but the baby's head would never turn to follow her movements. There was never a sign of recognition for anyone or anything.

When the baby was ten months old, Mrs. Fischer was forced with inexpressible grief, to face the fact that her baby could not see, and was deficient in every way. She could not sit; not hold her own bottle, nor turn over.

"However we laid her in her crib," says Mrs. Fischer, "that's the way she stayed."

The baby's head was globular in shape and enormous— 22 inches larger around than the normal sized head of a child the same age; and her face was disproportionately small. Her eyes were completely hidden in their sockets and turned upwards. As the mother puts it: "Her head was so huge that it just looked like a roof, and her eyes were clear back in her head."

At this time little Billie was taken for examination to an eminent brain specialist in Pittsburgh. She was tapped, and the original diagnosis of hydrocephalus was confirmed. The physician stated that the only hope for the baby lay in a brain operation. Surgery was scheduled for the following Tuesday afternoon. On the preceding day, Mrs. Fischer brought the baby to the hospital. She was again tapped, and her little head shaved of the fuzz that she had in lieu of hair, in preparation for surgery.

"It was some weeks prior to this," the mother recalls, "that I had begun to listen to Miss Kuhlman's broadcasts, and by the time I took Billie to the brain specialist, I had been to two of her services, so I knew what her ministry was all about."

Before taking Billie into the hospital early on that Monday morning, Mrs. Fischer had sent in a prayer request.

"On the Tuesday morning broadcast," says Mrs. Fischer, "Miss Kuhlman read this request, and prayed for my baby over the radio."

"Tuesday afternoon I went to the hospital to be there when Billie was operated on. The doctor met me and said, 'Something's happened to your baby. We're not going to operate today. We'll probably go ahead with it on Friday, so just leave her here, and we'll see.' "

On Friday afternoon there was no operation, either, and thus it went five weeks: each week an operation tentatively scheduled, and each week the operation postponed.

Five weeks later, Mrs. Fischer was to bring her baby home from the hospital—her head diminished in size by some ten inches, but still monstrously large. The doctors had said, "Let's wait a while longer. If this decrease in size continues, surgery will not be necessary."

But before Mrs. Fischer took the baby home, the doctors had given her what was perhaps the most shattering news she had yet received about her child. On the basis of tests given at the hospital, there had been made the diagnosis of a malady which no medical techniques could correct: her child was—and would remain—in the opinion of the doctors, hopelessly mentally retarded.

They urged her to make arrangements to send the child to Polk State School—an institution for retarded children. But the mother's instantaneous reaction was one of rebellion. She had six healthy, normal, unusually attractive children, but as seems inevitably to be the case in such circumstances, this small, blind, misshapen and mentally retarded child was, of all her children, the closest to her heart. She *could* not—she *would* not—send the child away to an institution; and she remained impervious to the doctor's warning that having such a child around in a houseful of normal children might very well have a bad effect on *them.*

"I just felt I had to risk that," Mrs. Fischer says. "All I could say to the doctor was: 'No. I can't ever send her away from me. I love her too much. And if she isn't aware of anything else in this whole world, she must somehow *feel* this love. As long as God gives me the strength to take care of her, I'm going to do it.' "

It was at this time that Mrs. Fischer decided to take the baby to every service at Carnegie Hall, praying with all her heart and soul that the healing hand of Jesus would touch this defenseless, defective baby, making her whole and perfect as she was meant to be.

But in seeking healing for this one child, she could not abandon the others. Thus the problem arose as to how she could attend the services and at the same time take care of the rest of her family at home. She happened to mention the matter to her oldest daughter, and the young girl immediately volunteered to go right from school each time and hold a seat for her mother. Not only that, but she announced to her mother that "I am going to fast, too— right along with you."

And thus week after week, they followed this procedure—the young sister holding the seat in the auditorium, while her mother fed her family at home, then quickly dressed herself and her little water-head baby, and took the long streetcar ride to Carnegie Hall.

After each service the child's head seemed to decrease a little in size, and after the first few weeks, everyone in the family began to detect changes, not only in her physical *appearance,* but in her physical *reactions.*

She began to try to hold her bottle. At first there seemed a scarcely perceptible impulse to move her hands toward it, and then on one memorable morning, she actually stretched out her hands for it, and they closed around it, and she lifted it to her mouth unaided.

And then one day her mother laid her in her crib for her afternoon nap. Mrs. Fischer was *sure* she had put the baby on her back, but when she went in the room a few moments later to get something she had forgotten, she glanced at the crib, and saw that little Billie was lying on her *stomach.*

At first the mother thought she might have been mistaken—that perhaps, after all, she had left the baby on her stomach when she left the room. She now turned her gently back without awakening her. When she went to pick her up after her nap, she found the baby again on her stomach—so now she knew. It had been no mistake— Billie could actually turn herself over.

As the weeks went on, and Billie's head continued, gradually, to grow smaller, her eyes were no longer buried in their sockets; they no longer appeared obscured by the once huge, protruding head, and they no longer rolled upwards. Perhaps the most thrilling day of all was the day that Billie looked at her mother with recognition in her eyes, and smiled at her!

Never, for one moment, had little Helen doubted that her baby sister would be healed by Jesus: and no one, not even the baby's mother, was more thrilled than her twelve-year-old sister to see little Billie's condition slowly but surely being healed through the power of God.

Little Helen never grew impatient; she never once grumbled at giving up all her after-school activities so she could go early to the service; she never once even intimated that she was hungry during her day-long fasts— probably because, like David, her desire was so intense that she felt no need of food.

Waiting three hours *before* each service in order to hold a seat for her mother; standing three hours *during* each service, helping her mother with little Billie—taking her little sister's bottle to the ladies' room to warm it if the baby grew hungry—this was the kind of *active* faith honored by God. He did not turn a deaf ear to these acts of faith offered by a little twelve-year-old girl.

The greatest power God has given to men and women is the power of prayer, but always remember, God has established the law of prayer and faith. Prayer is conscious of the need, while faith supplies it.

Prayer never obtains anything from God unless faith is present: and again, faith never receives anything from God unless prayer makes a petition. Prayer and faith work harmoniously together—both are necessary in their distinct functions, but are quite different to their nature. Prayer is the voice of the soul, while faith is the hand. It is only through prayer that the soul can establish communion with its Creator, and it is only through faith that spiritual victories are won.

Prayer knocks at the door of grace, while faith opens it. Prayer contacts God, while faith obtains an audience. Prayer makes a petition, while faith presses through the multitudes to touch the hem of His garment, and receives from His giving hand. Prayer quotes the promise, while faith boldly proclaims the fulfillment of that promise. God listened to the mother's prayers—and He acted in response to her faith.

No one but God knew the perfect faith in the heart of this little girl, and He honored it.

A few months later, Mrs. Fischer took her baby to the pediatrician at Allegheny General Hospital.

He was astonished at the change in the child's appearance, and even more so after he had examined her and found her seemingly perfect. He called in the brain specialist who had formerly taken care of her along with eight other doctors all familiar with the case. They, too, examined her, and were all equally amazed to find the child perfectly normal in every respect. The brain specialist was heard to remark: "The Man upstairs gets the full credit for this."

This child whose head was once nearly twice the size of normalcy, so grossly misshapen that some who looked at her had nearly fainted: this child whose eyes were once so hidden in their sockets that no one even knew their color—whether brown or blue: this child who was once so physically retarded that she could not turn over let alone ever hope to walk: this child whose mental tests revealed an incurable mental retardation—is now twelve years old. "She is the smartest of all my children," says her proud and grateful mother—"An 'A' student in school." And she is as pretty as she is smart. Her eyesight is perfect, as are her mind and body and coordination.

All the children in the Fischer family have a close relationship, one with the other, but the relationship of this little girl with her big sister who is now nearly twenty-five, is one of special and extraordinary closeness.

As Mrs. Fischer says: "God has drawn them just a little bit closer to each other than to anyone else."

God honored the faith of a twelve-year-old child. He touched, in His mercy, the defective baby who was her sister, and He made her whole in every respect that she might live and work to His glory.

"Behold, I am the Lord, the God of all flesh; is there anything too hard for Me?" (Jer. 32:27)

The answer is NO! At the heart of your faith—at the heart of our faith—is a person; the person of Jesus Christ, the very Son of the living God. His is the Kingdom, and the power; *all* power; the only limit to his power lies within you as an individual. His is all power—AND HIS SHALL BE ALL THE GLORY.

10

Rose
"Jesus Can Do Anything"

This is the only place in the book where we are using a fictitious name. As you read on, you will understand the extreme delicacy of the situation which makes this necessary. The woman involved is a member of a well-known family. She herself now holds a good position with unlimited possibilities, and we wish neither to embarrass her family nor jeopardize her own future.

Narcotic addiction is a tragic affliction which has long been of deep concern to me. When recently I received a series of three moving letters, written by a teenager on behalf of herself and her "gang", I decided it was vitally important to include Rose's testimony. I felt that by so doing, the many who are in the same situation as this group of teenagers—the many who, like them, are desperately seeking deliverance from the drug habit—will be helped.

The letters of which I speak were written on successive Saturdays, and came to me exactly the same day for three weeks running. They were all signed "X"—for as the writer said: "My mother and father are prominent people. They do not know that I take dope, and I can't disgrace them. So you see why I can't sign my name."

The first letter began; "I have wanted to write you for a long time, but I live in fear of everybody. But now, Miss Kuhlman, I just have to have help, so I decided since God helped you to help so many people, maybe I can get help too."

The writer was an eighteen-year-old girl who got in with the wrong crowd; and by "wrong crowd" she makes it clear that she does not mean, as she puts it, "a bunch of slum kids." All her friends come from nice homes, and as she says: "We all have good mothers and dads. It isn't *their* fault that we are taking dope."

It had all begun as a lark—a desire to have fun—but at the end of the year, these teen-agers found themselves "hooked". There was no longer any element of "fun" in their situation: it was stark tragedy. Realizing what had happened, they made tremendous efforts to "kick" the habit, but it was too deeply entrenched; they were hopelessly enslaved.

The girl who wrote the letter tells how inadvertently she happened to tune in to the broadcast. It struck a chord, and she felt for the first time in her young life the reality of the love and compassion of Jesus. She hardly dared hope—but perhaps—just *perhaps*, He in His mercy might help *her* and her friends.

She listened secretly at home every day for a week, her room radio turned very low; her bedroom door tightly shut, for she did not want her parents to know.

During those seven days her hope of deliverance grew each day, and she began to reason that if God could heal a cancer patient or an alcoholic, He could heal a dope addict.

She had been embarrassed and reluctant to tell her friends that she was listening to a religious program, but one day when they were all together discussing their terrible problem, she said, "Listen, kids—as I see it we have only one hope—and that's God."

At their look of surprise, she proceeded to tell them of the daily broadcasts and they all began to listen—sometimes together and sometimes alone in their own rooms.

"I pray," X wrote, "But I guess that I don't know how to pray right. If only we could come to you and have you pray for us. We want so much to come to the services," she went on, "but we are afraid. We are afraid of the police. If they should take us, it would disgrace our parents. We simply *can't* let them find out that we take dope. It would just break their hearts."

It broke *my* heart as I read on:

"I know you are of God, and I believe and have confidence in all you say. But I guess that doesn't mean much to you coming from a dope addict, does it, Miss Kuhlman? But someday soon I'm not going to be an addict any more."

She ended by asking me not to read her letter over the air.

"I am so afraid," she said, "but I will listen to your broadcast every day. Please pray for us all."

I prayed for them the following Thursday, and her next letter (a week later) thanked me.

"I want you to know how much your prayers helped,"

she said. "Last Friday I prayed the way you told us to, and I asked Jesus to forgive me and come into my heart.

"I believe He did," the letter continued, "but I still can't stop taking this dope. Please believe me when I say I have tried so hard, but still I can't stop. I don't want it but I have to have it. I am *so* afraid, but I don't know what to do."

X was greatly concerned over her mother and father. She loved them deeply and knew she was reaching the point where she would have to tell them.

"Mother knows already that something is wrong," she wrote. "But she does not know yet what it is."

Her birthday was the following Thursday, and she asked me to have *It Took a Miracle* sung over the air on that day. "This is the birthday present I want most," she said.

Her letter ended with the words:

"I know you are praying for me, and please *don't stop.*"

And I *was* praying for her, and for all of them, from the bottom of my heart.

Then came what was to be the final letter, telling me that she was moving with her family to another state.

"I will not write anymore to you," she said, "but remember, I will be listening to you every day. Your broadcast is all I live for, although I've never seen you. If only I had dared to come to a service!"

And then she asked the question which has led to this chapter: "Has anyone ever truly been delivered from dope in your meetings?"

In answer to her query, I present the story of Rose as it actually happened. The only thing not factual is her name.

It was a Miracle Service, one Friday afternoon, when I suddenly became aware of the fact that a young lady was walking from the back of the auditorium down the main aisle—at first slowly, and then after reaching a certain distance, she almost ran.

Not expecting the incident, I stood watching the young woman, wondering just what she was going to do and the cause for her action.

When she came to the front steps leading to the platform, instead of walking up those steps, she stopped directly in front of the first step and dropped to her knees, seemingly unconscious of anyone else in the auditorium, she was not even aware of my presence. Covering her face with her hands, she began to sob until her entire body shook with emotion—the tears running down her arms and dropping on the steps before her. As long as I live, I shall never forget this sight, for if ever I saw a penitent soul—if ever I witnessed real sincerity—if ever I saw *desperation*—it was at that moment.

Slowly I walked to where she was kneeling, and we knelt together. In that moment I felt that any word I might speak would be superfluous, for already she had made her contact with God. Tenderly I put my arm around her shoulder and spoke quietly, "What do you want Jesus to do for you?" My question was answered with just one word: "Dope!" she said no more.

We were both totally unaware of the fact that there was anyone else near us, and in that moment it was as though Jesus himself became so real that all we needed to do was to reach out and touch Him. And then softly I said to her, "You and I know that Jesus can do *anything*," and she answered. "That is why I am here."

Continuing, I said, "I'll pray a simple prayer, and you pray it after me, and when you pray these words, mean them with all your heart.

"Dear Jesus, I confess I am a sinner," and she repeated the words after me.

"I throw myself on your mercy—please help me! I give myself to you completely—take away this desire for dope—take it out by the very roots." Each time she repeated the sentence firmly, distinctly and with a relinquishment to God which could not be mistaken. By the time she had finished the last words of this simple prayer, she had ceased crying; there was no more sobbing; there was no emotion—the transaction had been completed—and we both knew it.

That was absolutely all that anyone standing near could have seen or heard. But a transaction had taken place which was witnessed by all of heaven, and I believe that even the very angels witnessed that scene, for the greatest transaction that a human being can ever experience, had occurred. The very thing that Jesus died for had taken place in the body and in the life of that young woman: She had been set free not only from sin, but from the very *power* of sin.

I am quite sure that this entire experience took no longer than five minutes, and with the mascara smeared on her face, she stood looking like an angel. Quickly and spontaneously, I laughed and said: "You look like a different person"—and just as spontaneously she replied: "I *am* a different person!"

With assurance, with confidence, with the knowledge of forgiveness of sins, and with a complete sense of her release, I stood and watched her as again she walked down that main aisle and up to her seat in the balcony, from where she had come.

We continued with the Miracle Service. Little did I know the story behind that marvelous experience: little did I know that kneeling there that moment was a young woman who had been in every hospital in Pittsburgh with the exception of one. And not only had she been in each of these hospitals not once but several times, but she had also been committed to Mayview State Hospital near Pittsburgh, where she had undergone treatment for nearly a year.

The ten long years of her addiction were a living nightmare. She *wanted* to stop but was powerless, even with all the medical help she had received. Each time she went into the hospital, she entered with the full understanding of the doctor regarding her drug addiction, and God knows the medical profession did everything humanly possible to cooperate and help.

It had all started out so innocently with a simple cold which had hung on too long. A friend who happened to hear her cough said, "I've got something that will stop your cough right away."

She handed her a small bottle of medicine. And that was the beginning.

The "something," loaded with a narcotic, relieved the cough and relaxed her nerves—so she got more from the friend. By the time this was gone, Rose found herself irrevocably "hooked." For the next ten years she was to be a dope addict.

A young, unmarried woman, Rose soon lost the excellent position which she held because of her "nervousness" and unreliability. In the early part of her addiction, she tried to work, for she neeeded the money to buy the drugs, but although she got several jobs, she could hold each for only a few weeks. Finally she gave up trying and withdrew from reality completely, spending a good part of her time locked in her room.

Rose, whether she was working or not, managed somehow to get money, as all addicts do, for the narcotics, and like all addicts, she soon got to the point where she could stop at nothing to get them—often pilfering money from a relative's purse while she slept.

Her doctor signed her into an institution on two separate occasions, but as this was not a formal commitment by her family, she was at liberty to leave when she chose, and she "chose" after a few days each time. Because of the status of the family, and their connections, she was at no time formally committed to these institutions.

Meanwhile her condition continued to deteriorate in every way. She could not eat, and had lost over thirty pounds. She had by now retreated from the world almost entirely, refusing to associate even with members of her own family, who, aware of what was wrong with her, tried to shield and protect her.

Finally, upon her doctor's urgent advice, plans were made to have her institutionalized for the third time. This time, however, she was to be formally committed by her family, and she would not be permitted to leave until she had received the full course of treatments.

The papers were duly drawn up, and awaited only the doctors' signatures which were to be procured on Saturday morning. At that time she would be immediately committed.

The afternoon before the scheduled commitment, she came to the service, knowing full well that God was her last hope—the only ray of hope left—before her formal commitment for narcotic addiction. That was the reason she was so desperate: it was virtually a life and death matter with her when she walked down that aisle of the auditorium and knelt at the bottom step; that was the reason she was completely oblivious to the crowd, for Jesus was her only hope, and if He failed her, she had nothing left.

God saw what no human being could see: the sincerity, the willingness, the surrender, the desire—with every atom of her being crying out to Him for help and deliverance.

"Like as a father pitieth his children, so the Lord pitieth them that fear him."

The physician looked puzzled, and then he asked, "You mean she has no withdrawal symptoms? *Nothing?*"

"There is something queer going on in that auditorium! I have a patient who had been a bad alcoholic for years, and he was instantly delivered the same way. I guess what it boils down to," he continued, "is that God can do anything."

When the doctor at the institution had been informed regarding that which had happened, he was astonished. "This is the most wonderful thing I have ever heard," he said. And then he added ominously: "But she'll be back."

That was five years ago, and Rose has not "been back." Since then, she has had free access to narcotics at a local hospital during the time that she was employed there: she was not even remotely interested, let alone tempted.

It was a moment of extreme emotion and deep gratification, when I received a letter from a state senator—a long and dear friend of Rose's family—for the letter was most unexpected. It said in part: "As a token of thanksgiving to Him, for the miraculous healing of Rose, will you please accept this Bible upon which I took my oath of office?"

11

Mary Schmidt

Love—the Greatest Force in the World

"Would you believe that a few days ago this woman had a goiter so large that it threatened to strangle her?" I asked the congregation.

Standing by my side was Mary Schmidt, who had suffered with an extremely large growth in her neck for over thirty-five years. It was so large that it protruded beyond the level of her chin, giving her an extremely grotesque appearance.

It was shortly after her husband died that Mary Schmidt attended her first service. To be sure, she badly needed the healing of her body, but she had a far greater need: the healing of her shattered spirit and broken heart.

No part of her body was free of the effects of her huge goiter, and least of all her nerves, which had long been in very bad condition due to her affliction.

Her husband had died a sudden accidental death, and this additional nervous, as well as emotional, shock threatened to prove to be too much. Physically ill, despondent, so nervous that she was nearly out of her mind, she felt that she could not face the lonely, sick, purposeless life that lay ahead of her now. There came the time when she could see only one way out of a future which seemed intolerable: suicide.

And yet she fought this impulse toward taking her own life. Brought up in the church, she knew in her heart that self-destruction was a great and perhaps unforgivable sin. And yet the fear which possessed her—the fear she felt of life and everything it held for her, seemed more than she could face. Again and again recurred the thought that only death could give her release. She had become afraid of *everything*. So fearful was she at night, that every evening a neighbor or friend sat with her for hours at a time trying to calm her.

One night in November as she paced the floor, distraught, afraid and in despair, she remembered the words of a neighbor: "Why don't you go to the services at Carnegie Auditorium?" she had said. "You'll find help there, I know. I was cured of polio, but more than that, I found the Lord."

When Mary had first heard those words, they didn't register at all. She went regularly to her own church; why go to a religious service way over on the North Side?

But now, she wondered. She *had* to find some help somewhere. She *had* to have some help—something to hang on to—or she knew she simply could not go on.

Next morning found her on a streetcar on her way to Carnegie Hall.

When she got off the car in front of the auditorium, she was amazed, and slightly nonplussed, at the size of the enormous crowd gathered there waiting for the doors to open. She wondered, but she walked up the steps to join them. And she says, "I thought I'd never get to the top. I felt as if I were climbing a high mountain. My legs hurt badly; I had great trouble breathing, and my heart was very bad. By the time I got to the top of those steps, it was pounding so hard and I was so breathless, I thought I would collapse before I could get inside the doors which were just then opened."

She was astonished and upset at what she saw. Used to an orthodox service, she had never heard of the "power of God," let alone seen it at work, and as she saw person after person struck with this power, she watched wide-eyed with amazement, not knowing what to make of it all.

And then a peculiar thing hapened. As she watched, standing in the back of the hall, she felt something go through her from the top of her head to the soles of her feet. It felt like some sort of chill.

"I've had enough of this place," she thought to herself, "and I've got enough trouble without getting chills here."

She looked to see if she were standing by a window that might be open, but there was no window anywhere near her. The door she stood beside seemed tightly closed, but she moved away from it, thinking perhaps that a draft from it was making her cold. She moved away, but the chill continued—a chill hard to describe for she had never felt its like before.

As she says now, "Of course this was the power of God touching me, but I was so ignorant then of spiritual things, I had no idea what it was at that time."

Then she heard her first sermon on salvation.

"I had never heard of anything like that before," said Mary, "although I had gone to church regularly. When Miss Kuhlman spoke of being 'born again,' I couldn't understand that, either. I figured I was certainly in the wrong place for me, but as long as I was there, I decided to stay to the end.

"And then," Mary continued, "Miss Kuhlman told us to kneel down and repent. I didn't know how to pray this way, and I didn't know what to say, but I thought to myself 'At least I can cry, and no one will see me.' "

Mary dropped to her knees, and the words came, simple, short, and from her heart: "Oh, Jesus, forgive me," she prayed.

And when she arose from her knees, she had experienced her first miracle of God's mercy, for in that instant she knew that she had lost all fear forever.

When she went home that night, a neighbor came over as usual to sit with her.

"Thank you," smiled Mary, "but I am not afraid anymore. I don't need anyone to help me. I found my help this afternoon."

That night she slept the night through for the first time in many weeks—warm and secure. The next morning, she ate a hearty breakfast, enjoying every mouthful, and it all stayed down, also for the first time in many weeks.

The reason for Mary's whole emotional predicament— her utter hopelessness; her complete despair; her overwhelming discouragement, can be aptly expressed in one sentence—incidentally her own: "I went to church, but I still knew very little of the Bible; I knew *about* the Lord, but I didn't *know Him*."

She had begun to know Him very well at that first service. Mary now took her Bible and read it over and over again.

"I took it to the auditorium each time I went," she says, "and when Miss Kuhlman preached, I marked the chapters she mentioned, and when I got home I studied them, and could hardly wait to go to the next service!"

Mary had had her goiter for thirty-six years. It was sixteen and a half inches in width at this time. She was so short of breath, she could not walk up the smallest incline without stopping every foot or so to get her breath. Her whole body was involved and affected by the goiter. Not only was her heart extremely bad, but she suffered great pain in her arms and legs.

She and her husband had spent a small fortune on doctor bills, hoping against hope that some physician somewhere could help her, but no help was possible. The growth was so deeply rooted and so enmeshed in her glands, that to operate and remove it would have cost her her life.

Immediately after the death of her husband, she had gone to her doctor and pleaded with him to remove the growth: she didn't care then whether she lived or died. Her doctor, of course, refused to consider surgery, knowing that it would mean her certain death.

As Mary's knowledge of Jesus increased, she only wondered how she had lived so long without Him, and wondered how she could have thought of taking her own life—of wantonly destroying that which He had given. In the beginning of her spiritual awakening, her purpose in living may have been only to go to the next service. But before long, it was to serve God with her whole heart and life.

She had known nothing of the physical healing wrought by God when she attended her first service. In going that first day, her only thought was to find spiritual help. But now, as she saw so many marvelously healed, she grew in faith that she, too, could and would be healed.

Mary had now been going to the services for several months, and although spiritually she was vastly improved, her physical condition seeemed to be growing steadily worse. Her breathlessness had increased to the point where she could scarcely walk even on a level surface. It was becoming increasingly difficult for her to swallow, and her eating was already greatly restricted. She knew if God did not heal her, she would undoubtedly die from the goiter, as had her mother and aunt before her, from the same affliction.

On a Thursday in May of 1949, Mary went as usual to the auditorium. She had had a particularly bad and sleepless night, fighting for breath the whole night through. This day she took a prayer request with her to the auditorium.

The service was nearly over when she felt a terrific pain in the top of her head, and simultaneously she felt something pull and tug at her neck.

Instinctively she put her hand to her throat. *There was no sign of the goiter!*

"Oh, Lord," she said, the tears of joy and gratitude streaming down her face, "Is it *really* true?"

It was.

She kept feeling her neck, and then she ran back (no breathlessness now!) to the ladies' lounge to look in the mirror. She hardly knew the woman she saw reflected there; for thirty-six years she had seen a huge, misshapen neck, and now it was normal and shapely.

As Mary says, "For the next three days I couldn't sleep or eat, I was so thrilled. I wasn't sleepy; I wasn't hungry; all I could do was to keep feeling my neck, and looking in the mirror, and thanking the Lord."

When Mary returned to her doctor, he was astounded. "What happened?" he exclaimed.

"Do you believe in prayer?" Mary said.

"I most certainly do," came his answer. And Mary told him what had happened.

He examined her carefully and found her in perfect health; the heart condition which had badly worried him, completely gone along with the goiter.

This same doctor was to ask many times for prayer.

Today, thirteen years later, Mary Schmidt is a physically well woman, working five days a week. As she says, "I can breathe; I can sleep; I can do any amount of work and never have any bad effect."

But far more important, Mary is a spiritually transformed woman. For now she not only knows *about* Jesus, she *knows Him.*

There is in these displays of divine power a divine tenderness and gentleness more impressive than the miraculous element itself, revealing divine sympathy and divine love and indeed divine authority!

The world would have us believe that the greatest power known to man is force; the Lord has proven that the greatest force in the world is love!

12

Bill Conneway
"Lord, Here I Come!"

He had been left for dead. The bullet had gone completely through him.

It was long before daybreak and bitter cold on the December morning in 1944 when the patrol started out. There were seven in the group, led by nineteen-year-old Bill Conneway, and their mission was to destroy trucks and cannons before they were overtaken by the enemy, due to sudden breakthrough.

Mission accomplished, and not yet daylight, the men were on the return trip. When they got within several hundred yards of their own line, three of the group went ahead acting as scouts to see if the way were clear. It was, as far as they could see, and they waved the others on. Bill and his three companions had just started across the field when it happened. Out of nowhere came a hail of bullets.

One tore its way through Bill's hips, tearing cartilages, nerves and muscles, as it plowed across his body from the right side were it had entered to the left where it finally emerged. The impact of the bullet spun him around crazily, and threw him hard to the ground.

When he came to, he found that another member of the patrol lay beside him, with both his legs shot off. Bill spoke to him in a low voice, but there was no response. He raised his voice and spoke again, and then he saw that the boy was dead.

Bill lay there, paralyzed—freezing and in excruciating pain. His wound, the size of a silver dollar, was bleeding badly, and he knew that if the blood could not be stanched, he would bleed to death before help came—if it *did*.

Being on patrol, Bill carried first-aid packs including sulfa. With almost superhuman effort, he managed to open these, and put one on each side of the wound— "more or less stuffing it in," as he puts it, "to stop the flow of blood."

Hour after hour, his dead buddy beside him, he lay there. There was no sound; no sign of any living being. As the day wore on, Bill prayed as he had never prayed before. "I expected to die out there," he says, "and everything I had ever done in my life came before me." And there was plenty of time to live his life in retrospect, for he was to lie there all that day, and all that night, and part of the next day—endless hours which seemed like a thousand pain-racked, fear-filled years.

Lying there on the ice-brittle grass, desperately wounded, Bill had all but given up hope, when suddenly he heard the sound of approaching voices. His spirit soared, and he started to call out, but the words died in his throat—for as the voices drew nearer, he recognized the guttural syllables of their owners. They were not Americans, but Germans.

The first thing he knew, a heavy body was lying across his face, threatening to smother him. The German leader had tripped over the young American patrol leader, hidden as he was in the tall grass.

The moment that Bill had recognized the German voices, he had virtually abandoned hope of rescue—for he knew the Germans were not taking prisoners at that time. He braced himself for the inevitable. He fully expected to be shot where he lay.

The German sergeant picked himself up, looked hard at Bill, then called to the others in his group. They argued vociferously for several minutes. Bill didn't understand German, but every once in a while he caught a word, and as he says, "It was obvious that some of the men didn't think they should pick me up."

After what seemed an interminable time but could not have been more than five minutes, the sergeant, who outranked the others in his party, silenced them. To Bill's surprise and joy, he gave an authoritative order not to shoot, but to pick Bill up.

The men of course had no litter, so one of them grabbed Bill's legs, and another his shoulders, and carried him back into a school building where there were a few British soldiers and three or four other Americans.

No medical aid of any sort was given the badly wounded boy. "I don't think they had any to give us," Bill says.

And then he was loaded into a boxcar and taken to a German prison camp.

From December 21 to the end of May, he was shuttled

from one prison camp to another. During these five months no medication whatsoever was given. There was never more than one well for three thousand men, so water was strictly rationed—a quart a day. Bill drank only enough to keep alive—the rest he used to wash out his wound. Miraculously no infection developed, and although the wound did not heal, it drained the entire time. Doctors were to say later that it was this draining process which saved his life.

When it rained, the men had enough water to wash, but for five months they did not shave. "Occasionally," relates Bill, "we would cut each other's hair with a sharp stone or any old piece of tin we would happen to find lying around. We'd just take a fellows's hair and hold it up in our hands and snip it off. We'd all be bald on top, with the hair around our ears as long as ever."

When the Russians liberated the Allies held in German prison camps, Bill was then sent to a Russian camp where the situation remained remarkably the same.

"They would have been glad to do more for us," Bill says, "But they were given nothing themselves."

Their daily ration of food continued as it had been under the Germans. Their nourishment consisted of a water glass full of turnip soup every twenty-four hours. The men supplemented their diet of watery soup with grass and bark off trees, and as Bill says, "We were glad to get these things."

Fifty-five per cent of the men died from disease and starvation during those months, but Bill, terribly wounded, and with no medical treatment, managed to live.

The Battle of the Bulge claimed forty thousand American lives before the Germans were routed. It seems evident that there was divine purpose in the saving of Bill's. As he says now, "God was certainly with me all along."

When he got back to the United States more dead than alive, Bill weighed ninety pounds instead of 182. He was taken directly to the Newton D. Baker Hospital in Martinsburg, West Virginia, where he remained for three months.

He was no longer paralyzed, for this condition had lasted only sixty days, and although in continuous pain, he could walk—a fact which amazed his doctors. "I don't know how this is possible," said one after examining the X-rays showing the course the bullet had taken.

After dismissal from the hospital, Bill tried to go back to work at his trade of bricklayer—married in 1943, he had a wife to support—but the effects of his wound became more and more pronounced as time went on.

From the beginning, he had been unable to make a full cycle with his legs. He walked stiffly, dragging one leg, in an effort to gain relief from the constant pain. As he says, "I hadn't been one day without it since 1944." He had been in and out of hospitals several times, but nothing could be done for him.

And then arthritis of the legs and spine set in, and the pain was just that much worse, especially in his back. He was in near desperation. For now, in addition to his wife Thelma, he had a small daughter Susan to take care of, and he found himself virtually unable to work. To sit—to lie—to stand—all caused agonizing pain in his spine.

In 1955 he was hospitalized again, and he was now told that in addition to the arthritis, he had a ruptured disk. An operation to relieve the pain was advised. But this is a tricky operation, and taking into consideration the rest of his condition, Bill was given no assurance that he would be substantially better after surgery. He was not ready at that time to take the gamble of surgery where the outcome, in his case, was clearly unpredictable.

Feeling that if the arthritic condition in his back and legs were improved, the pain might lessen to the point where he could do at least a limited amount of work, Bill went to Arizona for a brief stay—hoping the warm dry climate might do the trick.

And when he returned to his home in Elizabeth, Pennsylvania, he *did* seem better for a little while. But bricklaying is a strenuous job, and he had pushed himself too far and too hard from the first. In June of 1956, "my whole back just seemed to collapse," he says.

Even lifting his arms caused intense pain, and he could not bend or twist his body at all. He had not been able to drive a car for many months, but now he could not even get in one unless he crawled in. He could not bend his head sufficiently to get in the door.

He could not stand on his right leg at all, nor could he remain in an upright position for more than a few minutes at a time, without having to lie down. He could not sleep in a bed, regardless of the plank under the mattress he had used for twelve years to make it firm. He had now to lie on the floor. To sit in a chair was of course absolutely impossible.

In July he was taken to the Veterans Hospital in Clarksburg, West Virginia, where he was kept flat on his back for five weeks. At the end of this time, he was told that although no guarantee of success could be given, there was no alternative but to have surgery performed. Bill by this time was willing to try *anything* with *any* chance of alleviating his pain, and thus enable him to work again.

He was given, at his request, a thirty-day pass before the scheduled operation in order to attend to matters at home before the surgery took place.

Before he left the hospital, he was fitted with a brace and told by the doctors on no account to take it off. His body was a good three inches out of line, and without this rigid support he would fall over to the side as though his backbone were nonexistent. He was further instructed to lie down most of the time at home, never walking more than a few minutes at a time. Above all he was cautioned to stay out of cars. In this condition he returned home to stay before the fusion operation was undertaken.

His wife, naturally enough, had for a long time been extremely distressed and worried over her husband's condition.

She had listened often to the broadcasts and attended several services. A woman of great faith, Thelma was convinced that Bill could be healed by God. But Bill "just didn't believe in such things"—and she could not get him to listen to even one broadcast, let alone attend a service.

It was on September 9, 1956, a week to the day before his thirty-day leave from the hospital was up, that a friend of Bill's stopped by, a friend who had been to many services, and knew a great deal about prayer and the power of God to heal.

It was before daybreak on the Sunday morning that he came by the Conneway home. It was obviously not a social call at this hour of the morning. It had been made with only one purpose in mind: to take Bill—whether or not he wanted to go—to the service that day at the Stambaugh Auditorium in Youngstown, Ohio.

It was very early in the morning, to be sure, but Bill was

not asleep because he *couldn't* sleep from the pain. He was lying, scarcely able to move, on the living room floor. Al was a close friend, and when he came in, Bill was glad to see him, but he was definitely *not* pleased at the prospect of going to the service.

"I had always said my prayers," Bill says, "But I wasn't much of a Christian, and I had no faith whatsoever that I would be healed. All I could think of was that three-and-a-half hour drive to Youngstown. I was in enough pain as it was without undertaking *that*."

His friend's insistence, however—his complete faith in the power of God to heal—finally persuaded Bill, and he got himself ready to go, however reluctantly.

Thelma, ill at the time, did not accompany them, much as she wanted to. She and their ten-year-old Susan stayed home, both agreeing to fast and pray throughout the day.

The drive was fully as bad as Bill had anticipated. Having to sit so long was almost unbearably painful. Then they got to the auditorium a good two hours before the doors opened in order to get a seat. They waited in the car, which meant another two hours of acute discomfort. During most of this time Bill stared at the steep steps leading up to the auditorium, wondering how and if he could ever make them.

When the doors opened, Al half lifted his friend out of the car. With help, Bill slowly, slowly, made his way up the steps which he had so dreaded.

They found two seats in the seventh row, and Bill's next problem was how he was going to manage to sit through the four-hour service.

"It was in the middle of the service," Bill says, "that I

started burning all over me, just as if I were on fire. And then I felt violently nauseated."

Bill didn't know what had happened to him, but his friend did. Al looked at him, and saw that the power was going through his body. "Has the pain gone?" he asked, smiling, a few minutes later.

Bill looked startled, and with his face as white as a sheet, just nodded.

"Come on," said Al, "we're going to the men's lounge to take off your brace." Bill hesitated—drew a deep breath—and with his friend, walked pain-free, for the first time in twelve years. He was aghast at what had happened, but definitely apprehensive and dubious at the thought of taking off the brace in view of the doctor's admonition not to remove it under any circumstances.

Nevertheless, both shamed and fortified by his friend's unqualified faith, he sat in a chair, and as he undid the brace, he said to himself, "Lord, sink or swim, here I come."

The brace was off, and Bill did not fall to the side as he had previously done. There was no doubt *now* that he had a spine—for he sat straight as a ramrod. And he *sat,* without any vestige of pain or discomfort. The miracle had been wrought!

He walked briskly back to the auditorium, and I watched him as he came toward me, his face radiant. He raised his arms. He ran down the aisle. He bent and twisted his body in every conceivable position. He ran up and down the steps of the platform, without any sign of pain. He stood then on his right leg which a few minutes before could bear no weight on it, and this leg perfectly supported the weight of his entire body.

He had been perfectly and instantly healed by the power of God. Bill Conneway, who says in retrospect, "It wasn't *my* faith. It was the tremendous faith of my friend, and my wife and little girl at home fasting and praying, and all the people in the auditorium each praying for everyone else.

"This has made me realize," Bill says with a new found wisdom, "That every one of us has a great responsibility for others—for the people around us are often more responsible than we ourselves, for what happens to us."

Bill couldn't wait till he got home to tell his wife: he called her long distance from Youngstown. When she heard his voice, her first question was, "Did you receive it?" And he said, "Yes—I *certainly did!*"

"When he told me that," Thelma says, "Susan and I started to cry, and we just cried and cried with joy."

They could hardly wait until the car came home, and then finally it drew up in the driveway. Bill got out quickly, walked into the living room, and sat on the *low footstool.*

"And," smiles Thelma, "he talked all evening, and he's not much of a talker!"

The neighbors say he has been talking ever since!

Bill had a week left on his pass before he was to return to the hospital—only not now for a ruptured disk operation, but only to check out! During this week he led a perfectly normal life, washing the car, driving it, mowing the lawn, and doing countless other chores around the house.

He walked into the Veterans Hospital September 16, carrying his brace. As his physician started to remonstrate with him because he wasn't wearing it, Bill interrupted, "Look, doctor," he said, "I don't need it."

The doctor, incredulous, carefully examined him and said,"By golly, you're right! There's nothing wrong with you at all. Go on home!"

Within a week after this, Bill Conneway had a full-time bricklaying job, and he has had one ever since.

Since his healing he has been examined by insurance doctors who assert he is in perfect physical condition, and several years ago he made an appointment with one of the top neurologists in Pittsburgh, who did not know him or his history and had never seen him before. This physician gave him a clean bill of health, and then Bill told the doctor the story of his former condition and his miraculous healing. The neurologist just shook his head and said, "The Physician who took care of you certainly knew what He was doing."

Six years later, Bill Conneway says, "You know, everything about me changed when God healed me, except my name. I only wish it hadn't taken me thirty-one years to find out what God can do."

What happened to Bill on that Sunday in 1956 was far more important than the mere healing of his body, which was and always is secondary to the far greater spiritual healing. You cannot have the power of God go through your body without it changing you as an individual, without it doing something to you on the inside. And this is by far the greater miracle.

"I am going to live for Him from now on," said Bill immediately after his healing, and he has kept his vow.

He gives unstintingly of his time and energy to witness to the power of God, and it is a thoroughly convincing witness in every respect.

He goes to church regularly now with his wife and

daughter, and his home is a truly Christian home, every member in it filled with love for the Lord.

Bill knows that his body as well as his soul belong to God. He knows, too, that conversion is more than letting Jesus come into your heart. It is giving Him not only your heart but also your body, as a living sacrifice.

13

Amelia

"I Want to See Jesus!"

The four-year-old child had just arrived home from the Miracle Service. Upon entering the house she rushed up excitedly to the picture of the Last Supper.

"That's Him, Grandma," she exclaimed, pointing to the standing figure in the painting. "That's Jesus! I saw him over at Miss Kuhlman's today."

The small girl had been taken to the service that afternoon by her grandmother—one of the rare occasions that she had been taken out in public for many weeks, so appalling was her appearance.

Some eight months before, little Amelia had awakened one morning with what appeared to be patches of a wet rash on her arms and legs. Before the week was out, her entire body was covered with running sores.

The first doctor to whom she was taken diagnosed the

trouble as eczema. He prescribed treatment, but her condition continued to worsen.

As the days went on, the sores began to bleed badly, and her whole body had to be encased in cloths. No water could touch her, and she was cleansed as gently as possible, with oil. Her arms were wrapped in bandages, and unable to bend them, they hung straight at the child's side. As her grandmother says: "Her whole skin was cracked open. Blood and pus constantly oozed out. She was in continual pain, and it was torture for her to have the dressings changed. She screamed if anyone came near her."

It grew impossible to comb her hair, so covered with sores was her scalp. She had no eyebrows whatsoever and her eyelids had been eaten away with sores. Her ears were actually rotting away, and one ear seemed literally to be falling off, so devoured was it by disease.

In the early stages of her disease she had been able to play with other children, but now her appearance revolted them and not only did they shun her, they were not allowed by their parents to visit her.

Before her face and head became so badly ravaged, her mother had tried to take her on a streetcar, but even then no one would sit beside her, and were reluctant to use even the seats adjacent to her. Young as she was, Amelia was pathetically conscious of the horror she engendered in others. She did not know why people stared, then turned away with an expression in their eyes she did not understand. It made her intensely unhappy. She would often cry and say to her mother, "Why doesn't anyone like me?" until the time came that she was virtually never taken out of the house.

As long as she was able, she played around her own

home. When her mother let her help with the household chores to keep her occupied, she was pleased and proud. But even this had to be stopped as it became increasingly painful for the child to move and impossible for her to bend her arms.

Doctor after doctor was consulted. They disagreed on diagnosis, but were in unanimous agreement on one point; whatever the malady was, it was the worst skin ailment they had ever encountered in their practice of medicine.

Finally one of the physicians on the case suggested to the family that Amelia be taken to the cancer clinic. Her grandmother had said to him that day, "Prayer helps, too," and the doctor had nodded.

It was at this point, while awaiting an appointment at the clinic, that Grandma gave voice to a desire she had long felt: she asked permission of the child's mother to take Amelia to one of Miss Kuhlman's services.

A devout Roman Catholic, as was the entire family, the grandmother had become interested in the Kuhlman ministry through the radio broadcasts. She had herself attended several services at which she felt she had been greatly helped.

Amelia's mother not only granted permission to take the child, but also agreed to pray at home during the hours of the service on the following day.

The little girl had been brought up in a religious household, and she was a child of simple and complete faith in Our Lord and His ability to perform miracles. She went to the service that afternoon as the faithful go to Lourdes—confident and expectant that she would be healed so that she would not hurt any more and could play once more with her little friends: so that she could again go places with her mother and ride on streetcars and people would smile and want to sit beside her and not turn away with funny expressions on their faces, but above all, as she confided to her grandmother, "I want to see Jesus."

"When I asked my son to drive us to the service," the grandmother told me later, "he demurred 'You can't possibly take her into a crowd of people, looking as she does,' he said. But I replied, 'Certainly I can—that is what the place is for. *They* won't mind.' "

But Amelia's uncle was not so sure. He waited outside for them just in case.

Once inside the auditorium, even Grandma sought to cover the child's head as best she could with her coat so that those who saw her wouldn't be frightened—for as she recalls, "Her skin was now so badly cracked that you could lay a pin in each crevice. The scanty hair that remained on her head was stuck tight to her scalp, and her ears just hung, as though they were both ready to drop off."

Amelia and her grandmother took their seats that afternoon in the rear of the auditorium—both totally unknown to me.

During the singing toward the end of the service, Amelia poked her grandmother: "Look, Grandma," she exclaimed in loud tones, "I see Jesus up there!"

"Where?" her grandmother whispered.

Heads turned in the auditorium as the child said, "Up there! At the side of Miss Kuhlman! Look at Him—Jesus up there! And see—He has His hands out."

Her grandmother looked down at Amelia, and then she looked again, and her heart began to pound. The sores on the little girl's face were entirely dried up. There was no evidence of blood or pus anywhere to be seen. Her heart overflowed with joy and thanksgiving.

When they left the auditorium, Amelia's uncle was waiting for them. He took one look at the little girl and nearly fainted.

"When we got home," reports the grandmother, "she couldn't wait to tell everyone what had happened. The thing she told was how she had seen Jesus. The thing her family saw was how her sores were all dried up. Her father took one look and cried, 'A miracle!' "

"I said nothing to anyone—I just wanted to make sure that everything was all right before I said anything about it."

The following week Amelia was again taken to the auditorium. In the middle of the service, the scabs covering her face and head and body began to drop off. "They came off her like snow falling," her grandmother said—"and I was embarrassed—for they fell all over some lady's clothes. But most of all I was thankful, and the whole time I was praising the Lord."

Thus was Amelia completely and permanently healed. She was grateful to Jesus from the bottom of her little heart, but she was not at all surprised, for she had known all along that He could and would perform the miracle.

The little girl's skin was now flawless. There was no sign of a sore; no indication of a scab; no marks of any scarring. Within a short time her washed and combed hair made a golden halo around her radiant little face. Her eyebrows became full and well marked; her eyelids and ears were fully restored. One thousand people saw the condition of this child and witnessed her healing which the doctors call a miracle.

Amelia's case has moved me as much as anything that has ever happened in this ministry, and not solely because of the physical healing, of which I have seen so many equally remarkable, but because of her unquestioning faith; her unswerving certainty of the reality of the vision she had had of Jesus; and the tenacity with which she has clung, over the seven years since her healing, to her original story.

In the beginning, friends and neighbors, although they could not deny the healing, either accused the child of making up the story or accused the grandmother of putting the idea in the child's head.

Her mother and father were at first convinced that the whole thing had been a product of a child's over-active imagination. They talked to her at length and questioned her closely, but nothing they could say could shake her insistence that she had indeed seen the Lord.

She still comes often to the services and from time to time, I,too, have closely questioned her.

"Did you *really* see Jesus?" I asked again only recently to the radiant, lovely-looking eleven-year-old girl she has become.

Clear and firm came the reply: "Yes."

"And where was Jesus?"

"He was standing right over there by you!"

"What did He look like?" I queried once again.

"Like the picture of the Sacred Heart, and His arms were outstretched," she said.

"Are you *positive* you saw him?"

Her face aglow, she answered, "Oh, *yes,* it is the realest thing in my whole life!"

"How long did He stand there?"

"At least five or ten minutes," came her reply, "long after the singing had stopped and you had finished your prayer." She smiled then, as she said, "Oh, Miss Kuhlman, I'll never forget it as long as I live!"

The experience of this little girl was clearly not imagination or an hallucination or a delusion, but a true vision. To a tiny, faith-filled child of four, who wanted more than anything in the world to see her Saviour, Jesus had revealed himself.

To those who persist in believing that it is *my* faith which is in some way responsible for the miracles occurring under this ministry, and that *my* prayers carry more weight than the prayers of others, I offer Amelia's case as only one among many, in refutation of this totally mistaken notion.

I point out that at the time of this child's healing, I did not know that the child was at the service, and therefore did not offer a special prayer for her. I did not see her until *after* she had received her healing—when I heard a voice ejaculate, "Look Grandma, I see Jesus up there!" It was only then that I ran my eyes quickly over the auditorium to determine where that small but penetrating voice was coming from, and finally saw, in the arms of some woman, a little girl gesticulating in my direction.

It was through the prayers of this child, *not* mine, that the power of God was released. And it was in response to the simple faith of a little child, *not* mine, that Jesus lay His hand upon her small body. I pray with everything within me, that no one shall ever see Kathryn Kuhlman in this ministry, but only the Holy Spirit.

Dear God, give to us the simple faith that little children know—the faith to believe in the living person and power of Jesus: the faith to look for miracles upon this earth. For if we wear this simple faith like a cloak around us, we will be blessed as children are, and it is then that we will not only know ABOUT LIFE—we will know HOW TO LIVE LIFE!

14

Elizabeth Gethin
"Go and Tell This Story"

"I came as a skeptic"—those words of truth and confession came from the lips of a woman who is well known in social and medical circles, and equally well known today in the Pittsburgh Conference of the Methodist Church—for Mrs. Gethin is Spiritual Life Secretary for the Woman's Society of Christian Service.

Elizabeth Gethin attended the University of Pennsylvania in Philadelphia, and the University of Alabama in Tuscaloosa. She is also a graduate nurse from the Western Pennsylvania School of Nursing, with postgraduate work in pediatric nursing taken in Bellevue Hospital in New York.

She has taught pediatric clinical nursing; the Social Sciences in nursing, and was Counselor for Nurses at the University Hospital in Birmingham, Alabama.

With such a background, it is perhaps not surprising that when she attended her first service in July of 1955 she was skeptical of "miracles."

It wasn't that she didn't believe in God. She did. A devout church woman, a lifelong Methodist, extremely active in her church, she considered herself a good Christian and a firm believer in the power of prayer—that is, in a sort of generalized prayer to be answered in a general sort of way.

She had served on the Commission of Religion and Health for the Council of Churches in St. Louis, and she was quick to acknowledge that God heals through the aid of doctors and nurses and medicine.

What she did not realize was that anyone could be instantly healed by the direct power of God. She did not believe that He performed miracles of healing today similar to those which took place during Jesus' earthly ministry—for surely, she reasoned, what had happened nearly two thousand years ago was not applicable to this present scientific age.

It was actually because of her sister-in-law, Dolly Graham, that Mrs. Gethin was to attend, reluctant and unbelieving, her first Miracle Service.

Dolly had had a mild heart condition for many years, but in the fall of 1948 she suffered a severe illness which caused irrevocable damage to the already imperfect organ. When she was released from Pittsburgh's Magee Hospital that November, she had been told that she would be a semi-invalid for the rest of her life.

After getting home, she only wondered why the doctors had used the word "semi," for the slightest exertion left her scarcely able to get her breath, and even eating was a strain. She was forced to rest in bed most of the day, her husband carrying her up and down stairs for brief sojourns to the living room sofa. She slept on four pillows—practically sitting up in bed—and frequently during the night she would awaken coughing and spitting up mucus and blood from her lungs. Her pulse rate was 126 beats a minute, and she was taking digitalis to slow it down.

Dolly had been a music supervisor in the public schools, and she dearly loved music. Her main diversion during her largely bedfast days was in listening to all the music programs she could get on her radio.

One day she heard over the air what she describes as unusually beautiful organ and piano music. She settled back to enjoy it, when, "I heard a woman's voice saying, 'And have you been waiting for me?' I quickly switched the dial to another station," said Dolly, "for I would get back to that station every day to hear that music. Then one day I heard someone give his testimony over the air. I don't remember now what it was all about, but it caught my interest, and I began to listen to the complete broadcast."

Dolly had gone to Sunday school and church, but she had never heard of spiritual healing, and as she says, "I knew very little about God. I pictured Him as far away up in heaven, if there were such a place, and I was sure He wasn't interested in us here and now. And as for 'miracles,' she went on smiling, I guess after graduating from college I just considered myself too intelligent and too 'intellectual' to believe in such things."

But after listening to broadcast after broadcast, Dolly began to wonder if there were not something to these healings she was hearing about. She finally asked her mother if she would take her to Carnegie Auditorium.

131

They went together for the first time, a few weeks later.

"I had fasted all day," Dolly recalls, "and by the time we got out of the auditorium, I was so sick I didn't know what to do, but I had seen wonderful things happen before my very eyes."

When her husband asked her that night, with raised eyebrows, if she had been healed, she said, "I don't think so. But there is something happening there I don't understand, and I must go back."

The next day she felt better than she had in a long time, but as she says, "I wasn't ready yet for my healing. I was still too ignorant of spiritual matters."

Some time later, she and her mother went to a Miracle Service. During the service, a little mute girl for whom the vast congregation was praying, was instantly healed.

"I was smiling and very happy," Dolly relates—"When suddenly something seemed to take hold in me and I felt as though someone were squeezing me all over. At the same time a brilliant light seemed to come through the ceiling and I had to cover my eyes to shield them from the most dazzling brightness I had ever seen. I began to cry and cry. No one else had seen that light, and they didn't know what was wrong with me."

From that day on, Dolly was insatiably hungry for the Word of God. She listened to every sermon she could hear over the radio; she read her Bible for the first time in many years, and she started back to church.

She still couldn't hold a hymn book because it was too heavy, and someone else had to hold it for her, and she still couldn't sing more than a few words without gasping for breath. But as she says, "My healing didn't really seem to matter to me any more. I had found peace."

It was at this time that Elizabeth Gethin and her family moved back to Pittsburgh. According to Dolly, she prevailed upon Elizabeth to go to a service with her, because she and her sister-in-law had always been devoted friends and she wanted to share with Elizabeth what she had found.

According to Mrs. Gethin, she accompanied Dolly to the service because, as a nurse, she knew the full seriousness of Dolly's heart condition and felt it unsafe for her to go alone to the auditorium.

"She was under medication," Elizabeth relates, "extremely cyanotic and breathless. Remember, she had been under strict medical care for eight years for a severe and medically incurable heart ailment. I simply didn't dare let her go alone for fear she'd faint—I wanted to protect her from the crowd. I must admit that I was reluctant and a little impatient to have to give up a whole day catering to a foolish whim of Dolly's, to go to some sort of religious service which I knew I wouldn't like or believe in. But I felt duty-bound to take her."

It was in the very beginning of the service, when prayer was being offered for a woman with multiple sclerosis, that the power of God went through Dolly. Mrs. Gethin, her nurse's training coming to the fore, observed every minute detail of what happened. She watched first with scientific curiosity and then with awe, the transformation in her sister-in-law which was taking place before her very eyes. She graphically described how Dolly's fingernails instantly turned from blue to a healthy pink; how color flooded into her face as though a blood transfusion were taking place; how something like an electric current ran through Dolly's entire body, quite obviously healing and restoring her. "As I watched Dolly under the power," says Elizabeth Gethin, "I knew instantly that this was God, for Dolly is an exceedingly down-to-earth and unemotional person. Furthermore, the healing that I was watching *had* to be God—there was no other explanation.

"In those moments I knew that I had never until now had a true vision of Him. And as I saw the healthy color of Dolly's glowing face, it seemed that the Holy Spirit spoke to me and said: *'You are here so that you can go and tell this story.'* "

Dolly's healing, both physical and spiritual, had actually been a gradual thing. She had had much to learn of the things of the Spirit, and as she said, "Had I received my healing immediately, I don't believe I would have felt the need, or been so eager to do deeper into the ways of God."

It was as if, as she consecrated herself increasingly to God, and walked more and more in His light, she received more and more of His healing grace.

Day by day she received strength, and as she says, "When I came to the services, I received still more strength. It seemed that any time I put forth the effort to step out on faith, I received that much more healing."

The climactic completion of her healing took place on that hot July afternoon seven years ago. It was on that day which will live forever in both their memories, that Dolly and Elizabeth were to know the full transforming power of Jesus Christ.

"I had thought I was a Christian," says Elizabeth, "but I saw now that I had *never completely* believed. But from that moment on there has been no question in my mind that God hears and directly answers individual prayer.

Above all else, I know now that all things are indeed possible with Him. This knowledge has not only changed *my* life, but that of many of my family, and neither Dolly nor I can ever be the same again."

Remembering her own doubt, Elizabeth Gethin was sure that no one she knew would believe the marvelous event which took place that July day in 1955. But as Elizabeth says, "They have *had* to believe"—for Dolly has been enjoying perfect health for the past six years. She is now directing her church choir, and witnessing to the power of God any time and anywhere that she can help others. Her heart specialist, examining her after her healing, stated that she no longer needed medication and withdrew the digitalis. And her family doctor was to say. "Yes—I *know* what has happened to you. In many years of medical work, I have seen God perform many miracles."

But Dolly's dramatic healing was not all that was to convince the people whom Elizabeth knew, that something wonderful had happened. The miracle that took place that day in Elizabeth's heart, which in its own way needed God's healing as much as Dolly's, is no less marvelous, and scarcely less obvious to those about her.

She has never stopped obeying the injunction of the Holy Spirit given her that summer afternoon in Carnegie Auditorium. She has indeed "gone and told the story," and her witness has been, and is, an inspiration and source of encouragement to Healing Services already existing and especially to new ones contemplated, in a number of churches in the Pittsburgh Conference of the Methodist Church.

But although her efforts to glorify God and to advance His Kingdom, had sprung initially from her sister-in-law's healing—they have not been confined to her *spoken* testimony as to the power of God.

"One of the most wonderful things about the healing," says Elizabeth, "has been the great avenue of prayer it has opened up."

For six years an interdenominational prayer group has met every Wednesday morning, mostly in the Gethin home; a prayer group, as she puts it, "where the Holy Spirit is the guiding power. Those who come—truly come with joy and thanksgiving, and with a spirit of great expectancy, wondering what God is going to do today. He has never failed us, but surely has answered prayer in a glorious way. We believe that joy and gratitude is the secret of a happy and successful prayer group."

As a direct result of this, there are now many such groups meeting weekly in prayer all over the city of Pittsburgh and vicinity.

Mrs. Gethin brings many of the prayer group members to the services, and among those marvelously healed by God has been her own sister, Jeanette, who was instantaneously healed of deafness while visiting here from Philadelphia.

Still another area has opened up through which Elizabeth and Dolly are working for the glory of God.

A few months ago, they both were inducted by the Rev. Alfred Price, into the Order of St. Luke, at St. Stephen's Episcopal Church in Philadelphia. This group of clergymen, doctors, nurses and lay people who believe in God's healing power, are working together to bring spiritual healing back into the organized church.

"I will never cease to be grateful to God for allowing me to see my precious sister-in-law healed that day in

Carnegie Hall," says Elizabeth Gethin. "That was the day that changed my whole world—for it was the day that I really came to know Jesus Christ not only as my personal Saviour, but as the Great Physician."

"Go home to thy friends," He said, "and tell them how great things the Lord hath done for thee" (Mark 5:19).

In her gratitude to God, Elizabeth Gethin is doing just that.

Precious Lord, how we thank you for the wonder of your love for us. You are our Saviour and our Lord. The great Healer of body, mind and spirit. Take us and use us, for the Glory of God—In Jesus' Name. Amen.

15

Amelia Holmquist
"It Was a Tender Touch"

They brought her in on a stretcher, her little body pathetically emaciated, but she was fully dressed! She was so certain that she was going to get off that stretcher—so *sure* that God was going to heal her—so *sure* that this was to be her day, that she had asked her husband to fully dress her before the stretcher bearers carried her out to the waiting ambulance. Amelia Holmquist was at this time totally disabled from arthritis; every nerve in her body was affected.

She was a Swedish Lutheran, but as she takes care to point out with considerable pride—and with an accent so thick that it is hard to understand her; "I am an American citizen"—and then after a short pause she adds, with a smile, "But I guess you might say that most of all, my citizenship is above—with the Lord."

It was some years before that Amelia noticed that her joints seemed stiff and swollen. When she was finally compelled by the pain to go to her doctor, he diagnosed the trouble as a form of arthritis.

He had prescribed the usual treatment—heat, massage, drugs, certain stipulated exercise to maintain normal joint function—but it all seemed unavailing. The pain continued and the stiffness increased. It became more and more difficult for her to lift and move her arms. She could lower herself into a chair with only the greatest effort, and once down, it gradually became physically impossible for her to get up. Her formerly brisk walk became a painful hobble, until she could not get around at all without the use of canes. All of her joints were by now grossly deformed, and the day finally arrived when she became entirely disabled and completely bedridden.

"It was at this point," she recalls, "that a neighbor dropped in to see me. She brought me a little red book called *The Lord's Healing Touch* written by someone named Kathryn Kuhlman, and she told me that Miss Kuhlman broadcasts over the radio every day, and to be sure to listen."

Amelia read the booklet and began to listen to the broadcasts, and as she says, another world opened up to her.

"I had gone to church all of my life," she says, "But until now I didn't know that God heals today as He did nearly two thousand years ago, and I never knew anything about *real* faith, until I read that little book and began to listen to Miss Kuhlman."

At this time Amelia Holmquist was completely helpless. She could not turn her head even a fraction of an inch nor could she move any part of her body. She was in almost constant pain, her entire body so sore that she could not be bathed with water, but only gently wiped with cotton saturated in oil.

From her normal weight of 145 pounds she was now down to ninety-seven pounds, and she was near death from exhaustion—the plight of about two per cent of arthritis victims in her advanced stage of the disease.

As she read and listened to the broadcasts, her faith began to grow. For the first time in many years, a conviction that she might again lead a normal life began to awaken in her long-hopeless heart.

One day, after listening to the broadcast, she asked her husband if on the following Sunday he would take her by ambulance to the service being held in Stambaugh Auditorium in Youngstown, Ohio. He refused—first because of his lack of faith, and second because he genuinely felt that the distance involved in the trip was too great to undertake.

"So then," Amelia says, "I began to pray to God that He would bring Miss Kuhlman closer to Akron, so I could get to her, and He answered by prayer. A month later a service was scheduled at Canton, Ohio, and I knew I could get there easily enough."

The ambulance was arranged for, and early that Sunday morning Amelia awakened her husband and asked him to dress her. He was aghast.

"Why?" he wanted to know. "People don't go places on stretchers in ambulances *dressed!*"

"Because," his wife said, her face alight, "I *know* that today is my day to be healed. I'll get up and walk away from that stretcher, and when I do, I'll have to have on some clothes."

Disapproving, skeptical, but in order to placate her as he would an unreasonable child, he proceeded to hunt in the closet for a dress that would button down the front—for she couldn't move her arms at all, let alone lift them up over her head. Finally he found one, and dressed her and combed her hair. She was ready just as the ambulance pulled up at the door.

They placed her carefully on the stretcher, trying not to inflict unnecessary pain. This was difficult to avoid, as there were only two small places on her back where she could be touched and lifted without causing great suffering. They then carried her out, and safely ensconced her in the ambulance with her husband beside her.

The ambulance was just about to start off, when she called to the driver, "Oh, wait—don't go yet. We forgot my *coat*."

Her husband looked at her incredulously. "Your *coat*," he said. "What on earth do you want your coat for? You're covered with blankets from head to toe!"

"Yes," she replied, "But I can't wear blankets when I go home. PLEASE GET MY COAT."

Staring at her for a moment, completely speechless, he went into the house and came back with her coat over his arm.

The attitude of Amelia Holmquist in this episode illustrates one of the fundamental requirements of divine healing; complete and unqualified expectancy that healing will take place. Amelia Holmquist possessed that important treasure that we call FAITH. This is not something we can take out and analyze; it is not something we can "work up." IT IS A GIFT OF GOD. "For by grace are ye saved through faith, and that not of yourselves, it is the *gift* of God" (Eph. 2:8).

We should all pray for this unspeakable gift. Because it *is* a gift of God, none of us deserves any personal credit for believing in Christ or for any faith we may have. We must give God all the glory, even for the portion of faith which we manifest and possess.

On that Sunday, never to be forgotten by either Amelia Holmquist or her husband, the ambulance drove up to the back door of the auditorium. The attendants carried the stretcher on which lay the helpless woman, and placed her on the platform.

"Perhaps I was healed even before I got to the auditorium," says Amelia in retrospect—"because I have no recollection whatsoever of being brought in. The first thing I knew, I was suddenly there on the platform, and I *knew* that if I could just get on that stage and stay there beside Kathryn Kuhlman, that God would heal me. I just *knew* He would."

As she lay on the stretcher, just as the service began, she had a vision. Now many people claim to have visions, and in my opinion the vast majority of them are imaginary, due to over-emotionalism, but this little woman—and I have observed her closely now for a long time—is one of the least emotional people I have ever met. She is a stolid, unimaginative individual, as well as one of great integrity. I can only believe that what she saw was real, and truly of the Spirit.

"Something made me look up in the corner of the auditorium," relates Amelia, "and even as I looked, I realized that the Lord had already loosened my neck; for the first time in many, many months I had turned it. I know now that there is a light in this corner, but to me, that day, there was no light. I saw instead something like a window, and there was a man standing there—I couldn't see his face—dressed in a white robe, and on a table beside him was a book in which he was writing.

"I'd never been to a service before," she continues, "so I didn't know what to expect. I turned to my husband and said, 'who is that up there, I wonder?' and he answered, 'There's nothing up there but a big light.' "

Amelia knew then that only she was privileged to see the Figure in the white robe.

"As I looked again," she went on, "I could see that all the pages in the book beside him were filled with writing. He seemed to turn and turn and turn those pages—one after the other—and it came to me that the book was about *me,* and that the pages were filled with my sins. And then, as I continued to look, all the pages seemed to become white. It was as if God had erased all my sins, and given me another chance to begin again."

That was Amelia Holmquist's first real sermon on salvation. I did not preach it; the Holy Spirit himself gave it. This was her sermon on being born again.

It was as Amelia had known it would be. After the Lord had loosened her head, enabling her to see Him, one of the women workers at the service went over to her and said, "Will you come with me now?"

She replied quickly, without thinking, "But I can't walk." And then she said, "Oh, yes I can! I *know* I can"—and in that instant she had the distinct sensation that someone had lifted her off the stretcher.

"It was a tender touch" she says in smiling recollection. "So tender!"

On her feet now, the worker brought Amelia over to me. She turned, and walked half way back, alone, to the stretcher, and back up again to me. I placed a chair for her on the platform, and she sat down in it with no trouble at all.

"For years," said Amelia, "I hadn't been able to sit until that moment. Then I got up by myself and started to the Ladies' Lounge. I couldn't find it, and in the looking I walked all over the auditorium, including down the stairs to the basement and back up again. All entirely alone."

This was the feat of a woman who thirty minutes before had been lying immobile on a stretcher, totally incapacitated: this was the feat of a woman about whom her doctor had said, "She will be incapacitated and in need of medication, for the rest of her life."

At the end of the service, the ambulance attendants came back to carry her out as they had brought her in. They gasped in astonishment and disbelief when they saw her.

Asking if she wanted to go back home on the stretcher, she replied in no uncertain terms: "No—I certainly don't. I'll ride up front"—with which she climbed up the high steps of the ambulance and proceeded to sit herself down. There was room for only three on the front seat, so one of the ambulance attendants occupied the stretcher on the ride back home.

Amelia says she couldn't stop talking all the way home, because she was so excited. The whole world looked so beautiful and new to her that she couldn't get over it. This was her new birth experience.

"From that day," she says, "I gave myself to the Lord, and I wouldn't have it any other way. I just love this life I

145

am living, and all things are so wonderful."

Getting ready for bed that night, Amelia questioned her thrilled husband.

"Remember," she said, "there on the platform at the service, when I first got up off the stretcher?" He nodded, "Well, who was it who lifted me up?" He looked startled.

"No one," he said. "No one lifted you. You got up by yourself."

She just smiled. She knew now why the touch she had felt had been so extraordinarily tender.

The next morning found Amelia out in the yard tending her rose bushes. Her next-door neighbor, seeing her from her breakfast nook window, came out and said, "It's uncanny. You look so much like Mrs. Holm—". And then she realized that she was Mrs. Holmquist.

White and shaken as if she had seen a ghost, all the woman could do was to keep on repeating, "I can't *believe* it. I just can't *believe* it!"

Since her healing, Amelia has not been sick a day, or taken so much as an aspirin tablet. In nearly ten years she has not had to consult a doctor.

This is a miracle of God—wrought by Him in response to the expectant faith of one of His children.

It is "Not by might, nor by power, but by my Spirit sayeth the Lord" (Zech. 4:6).

How well we know the truth of these words. From the bottom of our hearts we thank Him for these marvelous manifestations of His power and vow to give Him the praise, forever and ever.

16

Paul Gunn
No Case Is Hopeless

On the first page of the Sunday *Pittsburgh Press,* dated June 1, 1958, there was a headline: DOCTORS TOLD NOT TO SAY CANCER CASE IS HOPELESS. And now for the article:

"Doctors here were told yesterday to stop telling 'hopeless' cancer patients that their cases are hopeless. The *Pittsburgh Medical Bulletin,* official publication of the Allegheny County Medical Society, cautioned physicians against trying to be arbiters of fate, because nobody can say when anyone is going to die. Even when all the medical evidence indicates that there is no hope for a patient, the bulletin declared, the doctor must remember that the will of God, and little understood mechanisms in the human body, may intercede on the patient's behalf. The physiologic activities of the human body and the will of God, the bulletin stated, may permit the continuation of life and a certain degree of comfort and well-being in some cases where pathologic examination and clinical evidence preclude the existence of hope. Therefore, let us not be arbiters of fate and extend an absolutely hopeless prognosis although evidence of the same appears to be present, inasmuch as there are powers and factors beyond our ken, which may permit a reasonably comfortable existence in spite of incontrovertible evidence to the contrary."

It is not too much to believe that growing medical acknowledgement of healings such as that experienced by Paul Gunn, prompted the foregoing statements by the physician who was then editor of the medical bulletin.

Paul Gunn is a night watchman for many years employed by the Mesta Machine Company in Pittsburgh.

It was on September 28, 1949, that Mr. Gunn became ill with viral pneumonia and was taken to Presbyterian Hospital. There his condition failed to improve; his left lung did not seem to clear up regardless of treatment. His doctors grew suspicious, and ordered a series of extensive laboratory tests which were to include fifteen X-rays, two bronchoscopies and a bronchogram, plus three twenty-four-hour sputum tests. The findings of every one of these tests was positive, leading to an indisputable diagnosis: advanced cancer of the left lung.

The lung was too far gone to permit the use of non-surgical therapy—and the doctors ordered immediate removal of the infected lung and five ribs.

Paul did not need laboratory tests or doctors to convince him that he was desperately ill. His weight had dropped from 200 pounds to 120 pounds. He was constantly spitting blood during the day, and at night he would swallow blood in large quantities, passing it in the morning. He was in continual pain.

"My lung burned all the time," he recalls, "as though a blowtorch were inside me. I felt like a fire-eater at the circus. Every time I would blow my breath through my mouth, I was actually surprised that no flame came out. If anyone pressed on the left side of my chest, it felt as if the flesh were being held right down on a flame. I couldn't stand any weight, not even a Kleenex in my pajama pocket. I would set up and hold my pajama coat out from my chest."

While Paul was in the hospital, many friends came to see him. Appalled at his appearance and obvious condition, some of them mentioned to him the wonderful work that God was doing in the revival being conducted on the North Side of Pittsburgh in the Carnegie Auditorium.

"Divine healing was nothing new to me," said Paul, "so they really didn't have to sell me a bill of goods. I *knew* what God could do if we just put forth our faith. But faith without works is dead, so they asked if it would be all right if they sent in a prayer request to Kathryn Kuhlman."

This was not only "all right" with Paul, but he and his wife also sent in *their* request for prayer at the same time.

However, so bad was his condition by now, that his family did not expect him to live, prayers or no prayers— surgery or no surgery—until his birthday on October 23. And the doctors had made it quite clear that removal of the lung could not *guarantee* his recovery; it was simply the only indicated procedure that might conceivably save his life. Therefore to make sure Paul would have one more birthday celebration, his wife baked him a small cake and took it to his hospital room alight with candles, a whole week early.

The next day Paul inquired of his doctors how "immediate" his lung surgery must be. He was told that the operation *must* be performed within the next seven days. Were it to be delayed beyond this, the consensus of medical opinion was that Paul could not hope to survive.

Mr. Gunn then made an unusual request: sick as he was, literally more dead than alive, he asked to be released from the hospital for the week prior to the scheduled surgery. He asked this for two reasons: first, he had various business affairs he felt he must straighten up; and second and far more important, he wanted to seek God's healing—he wanted an opportunity to attend the services at Carnegie Auditorium.

The hospital cooperated, giving him permission to leave temporarily, and holding his bed pending his return in seven days for the operation.

The patient went directly from the hospital to his attorney, where he had his will drawn up, and then, straight from his lawyer's office he went to the Miracle Service on the North Side. It was only his unshakeable conviction that he would be healed which enabled him to withstand the pain in his chest, and gave him the strength to get to the hall.

"I hobbled in with two canes, so weak I could hardly stand—and in terrible pain," he says, "but the minute I walked in that hall I could feel the presence of God, and I knew He was going to do something for me. His Spirit was moving wonderfully there, and I knew what I saw that night were true works of God."

But Paul Gunn was not healed at that first service: "I

was too busy watching the rest," he says with a smile, "And praying for those who seemed worse off than I was."

Paul attended a total of four meetings that week, fasting and praying, and at the fourth service, after fasting for forty-eight hours, God touched him with his healing hand.

Some kind ladies had held a seat for him, so he wouldn't have to fight the crowds, and could come in just in time for the service. He was sitting in the fourth row, the fifth seat in, on that wonderful night. "I'll never forget any detail of it," he says.

"Suddenly the power of God came down. It hit me and just for an instant the sensation of burning fire in my lung was more intense than it had ever been before. I thought I couldn't stand it. It reminded me of the story of the three Hebrew children in the fiery furnace, with the furnace heated seven times hotter than ever before."

"And then," Paul continues, "It was all over—just like that."

"You know," he explains, "how when you light a piece of paper, it all crumbles up into ashes? Well, my chest felt as if a match had been struck to a piece of paper inside it. And then it seemed as if God had just taken His hand and touched the pile of ashes, and they all fell away, and from that moment on there was no more burning, no more pain, no more ache. And there hasn't been from that day to this."

This whole healing miracle had taken approximately one-half minute.

There was not the slightest doubt in Paul Gunn's mind as to what had happened: he knew he had been instantly healed by the power of the Holy Ghost. The date was October 27, 1949. He walked out of Carnegie Hall that night, upright and well. He no longer needed his canes for support, for he was strong in the Lord.

Two days later, Mr. Gunn returned to the hospital. His bed was waiting and surgery was scheduled for the next day. He had no need of either. He walked straight into his doctor's office, and claimed he had been healed.

Naturally enough, the astounded physician insisted on a thorough examination and a repetition of all the previously conducted laboratory tests—among them, more X-rays and another bronchoscopy were ordered.

"Before, when I had a bronchoscopy made," says Paul, "I would come down from the operating room bleeding profusely and would continue to bleed for a day, and each time after it was over, I felt I wouldn't live another two hours. Once when I saw my face in a mirror afterwards, I was *sure* I wouldn't.

"Two days after my healing, however, I walked in and undressed; crawled up on the operating table by myself; had the bronchoscopy done; and got down unaided off the table. There was not a drop of blood anywhere, and I felt fine!"

After the tests were completed, Paul walked the block down from the Presbyterian Hospital to Fifth Avenue, stopped in a restaurant for a cup of coffee, and walked a number of blocks to see a friend who had been in the hospital with him. From there he took a streetcar, went home, and that afternoon went back to Carnegie Hall to the service—this time to offer thanksgiving for his healing.

The results of the new laboratory tests were all negative—no sign whatsoever remained of the once deadly malignancy.

Within days, Paul Gunn was back at the Mesta

Machine Company, the doctor at the plant having approved him for work. He had been away three and a half months, and they had hired a replacement for him, but they took him back at his old job.

The first night back at work, two thousand men at the the plant came up and shook his hand, all grinning their congratulations. Not one had ever expected to see him alive again. One workman spoke for many, when he said, "That time I shook hands with you there at the hospital, I thought sure you were going to die while I still had hold of your hand."

Paul not only quickly regained his lost weight, but within a short time, had to diet to *lose* weight!

Long before he had ever developed cancer, he had suffered continuously from various aches and pains. Since his healing in 1949, however, he has never had a sick day, and he works eight and a half hours a night, six nights a week.

"If you take one step towards Jesus," says Paul, "He will take two toward you. Anyone at all can have anything from the Lord that they will believe God for."

Paul's glowing face is testimony to his convictions, and his wonderful witness which he has given countless times to innumerable people has brought many souls to Christ.

If it were necessary to prove his healing, he has in his home photostatic copies of his entire medical record with the exception of the X-rays taken, which are still at Presbyterian Hospital.

Two good examples of the state of his health lie in the fact that over the past twelve years, he has donated twenty-one pints of blood and taken out five new insurance policies. He has had every test known to medical science, and there is no evidence of cancer in his body.

In man's language, Paul's healing was a miracle, but the word *miracle* is not in God's vocabulary, for all these healings are a very part of His nature. They were paid for on Calvary.

When Jesus cried, IT IS FINISHED from the cross, He said, in other words, "It is all bought and paid for. It is at the Will-Call desk right now, for any man or any woman who will walk up and claim it."

Faith cannot be manufactured. One of the chief difficulties is our failure to see that faith can be received only as it is imparted to the heart by God himself. Either you have faith or you do not. You cannot manufacture it...you cannot work it up. You can believe a promise and at the same time not have the faith to appropriate it. *Belief* is a mental quality, but faith is spiritual...warm, vital...it lives and throbs and its power is irresistible when it is imparted to the heart by the Lord. It is with the *heart* that man believes unto righteousness.

"For I say, through the grace *given* unto me, to every man that is among you not to think of himself more highly than he ought to think, but to think soberly, according *As God hath dealt to every man the measure of faith"* (Rom. 12:3).

When we see the truth, we shall no longer be standing around poor sick folk hour after hour, rebuking, commanding, demanding, struggling...and because of our lack of the *truth* and the *Holy Spirit,* we bring a reproach on the Lord!

There is a place for intercession, but not in the exercise of faith. Intercession and the groaning of the heart may precede the operation of faith, but when God's faith is imparted, the only noise will be the voice of thanksgiving and praise.

The woman that had the issue of blood was not struggling to grasp a lifeline of deliverance by the power of *mental* apprehension; all she wanted to do was to get to Jesus.

All that the poor, miserable wretch on the Jericho road did, was to crowd into that heartrending cry the story of his own helplessness and his belief in the love and power and compassion of Jesus of Nazareth!

When God dealt to Paul Gunn his measure of faith it took approximately one-half minute for that faith to bring forth the result: a body completely healed of cancer by the power of God!

17

Richard Kichline

Healed by a Higher Power

The wife of the pastor of the First Evangelical and Reformed Church in Vandergrift, Pennsylvania, had just finished telling of the wonderful miracle in the life of her young son Richard, when a perfect stranger stood up in the auditorium and said, "Miss Kuhlman, I am sure that I am a stranger to the mother of young Richard, but I know that every word she has spoken is true. You see, my daughter was a nurse in the Presbyterian Hospital at the time this miracle took place, and she told me all about it, as it was happening."

On the fifteenth day of May, 1949, Richard Kichline, sixteen-years-old and a junior in high school, was stricken with paralysis.

It began one day when he stumbled for no apparent reason, and then seemed to have great difficulty in lifting his feet. When by the next day he seemed to lurch forward in an extremely peculiar fashion when he walked, his parents, Pastor and Mrs. Kichline, were very much alarmed. They called their doctor early in the morning and he came immediately, but after examining the boy, he seemed very puzzled and was able to make no diagnosis. Throughout the next twenty-four hours Richard grew rapidly worse, until by the third day he was not able to get out of bed: his legs were completely paralyzed and the awful malady was continuing its deadly work.

The Kichlines, praying that the doctor would be able to halt this dreadful thing, were in despair as they watched the paralysis continue to creep up in their son's body. Soon Richard could not hold even a tea cup. He was breathing, as his mother puts it, "only every other breath," and he had to be fed and cared for like an infant.

After two tragic weeks of increasing paralysis, a medical consultation was held, and Richard was subsequently taken by ambulance to the Presbyterian Hospital in Pittsburgh.

His mother, Laura, sat beside him on the way into Pittsburgh, while his father went ahead in their own car.

"He could talk," Laura said, "and his mind was just as clear as ours, but by this time the paralysis had traveled until it had reached his neck. He was totally paralyzed from the waist down, and by now was almost entirely paralyzed from the waist up."

The day after he was admitted to the hospital, his parents talked with the chief doctor there, and received the tragic news: Richard was a victim of acute transverse myelitis—a form of creeping paralysis.

This dread disease initiates in the brain, but the outward

manifestations are evidenced first in the feet. The disease works upward until it reaches the waistline; then it travels across the body to the vital organs above the waist. In the acute form of the malady, the type from which Richard suffered, death may take place rapidly from the extension of the disease to those portions of the spinal cord connected to the heart and the muscles of respiration.

In anticipation of such a contingency, an iron lung had already been placed in readiness should Richard require it.

The Rev. and Mrs. Kichline were completely stunned when the doctor revealed to them the seriousness of their son's condition. It seemed to them that their whole world had come to an end at that moment.

Richard was an only child—conceived and carried with great difficulty, years after his parents' marriage.

"He came to us," says Laura, "in answer to my longing and my prayer that God would give me a child, for I had been injured in an accident when I was a young girl and apparently could not have children. Finally I was operated on so I could have a baby and I remember to this day my joy when the surgeon said, 'Now you should be able to have the son you want.' Five years later Richard was born."

His birth was the fulfillment of his mother's long-held dream and deepest desire. She was never going to be able to have another child.

All the hopes and aspirations of both his parents lay in the sixteen-year-old boy, now completely paralyzed and in dire danger of unpreventable sudden death.

"What shall we *do?*" was Laura's anguished cry as she turned to her husband after receiving the medical verdict.

Before he could reply, the wise and kind doctor, to be

blessed for his Christian influence, answered her very gently, "You will have plenty of time for prayer."

He explained then that Richard would be hospitalized for the greater part of a year, and would then be taken to the D.T. Watson Home in Leetsdale, Pennsylvania for rehabilitation. It was only later that the Kichlines learned that their son was destined to be a paraplegic if he were to live, and this no one could say, for whether or not the heart would escape the ravages of the paralysis was unpredictable.

Laura Kichline had been a Christian since she was a little girl. At the age of eighteen she had fully consecrated her life to the Lord for whatever He would have her do or be. But not until a few months before her son was stricken ill, had she ever seen God's miraculous power actually healing broken bodies.

During the preceding November her husband had attended a service in Carnegie Auditorium, and as Laura puts it, "He came home greatly enthused, full of praise for Miss Kuhlman's ministry, and commented on the wonderful way in which God was using her." Therefore, when two months later a young friend in Vandergrift chartered a bus to go to Carnegie Hall, Laura decided to go along.

She sat in the balcony during the first service which she had ever attended, and in the beginning she was greatly puzzled by what she saw going on.

"I had never before seen the power of God visibly working," she said, "Of course I knew that God had worked marvelously in my own life, but I had never seen His power working in people's bodies as I saw here. There were many wonderful healings that night," she continued, "and I found myself praying with a fervor I had never

160

known before, for our church. I was unspeakably thrilled when I felt divine power go through my body while I was in the auditorium. I am sure now that God was preparing me for the sorrow and the bewilderment and the heartache which lay ahead."

And how beautifully He was to continue to prepare the way!

One evening as the Kichlines were having devotions, sitting by their sick son's bedside, Laura opened the Bible. Her eyes seem to be guided to Luke 1:37: "For with God nothing shall be impossible."

"I couldn't take my eyes off those words," she recalls, "it was as if God were actually speaking to me, and I remember saying and I think *aloud*, 'Art thou speaking, Lord?' "

He was—for on this night Laura was led to *believe* those words of Scripture with all her heart and soul.

As she says, "Had I not seen miracles of healing performed by the power of God in Carnegie Auditorium at Miss Kuhlman's services? These I knew, were no imaginary healings. They were the real thing. I had actually seen the power of God at work in His own masterpiece, little realizing at the time that in the near future we in our home would need His help so desperately."

That night Laura and her clergyman husband wrote to me, asking prayer for the healing of their son.

"Miss Kuhlman suggested," Laura relates, "that we agree in prayer on John 15:7—'If ye abide in me, and my words abide in you, ye shall ask what ye will, and it shall be done unto you.' "

"We held on to that promise, tight, claiming it as our own," she continues, "and although I can't prove it, by faith I take it, that when we began to really trust God and

161

rely on that promise, the paralysis stopped short of Richard's heart."

During these days Laura never missed a broadcast, and she fasted regularly—"For I had learned the value of fasting for spiritual things," she said, "when I had attended the service and saw the results."

The Rev. Kichline also knew well the value of fasting, but owing to a serious operation he had undergone in February, he was forced to try to build up his physical strength as rapidly as possible, a strength not only taxed by his ministerial duties, but by Richard's illness. He found solace in the fact that he could not fast during this period, in the words, "And that thou hide not thyself from thine own flesh" (Isa. 58:7).

As the Kichlines prayed together for Richard's healing, Laura diligently searched her heart, knowing "If I regard iniquity in my heart, the Lord will not hear me" (Ps. 66:18).

She made a vow that if God would see fit to answer their prayer, He would always be given the glory.

It was in the morning of a day late in June that God, through His Holy Spirit, acted in response to much prayer and great faith.

Richard lay supine in bed, as he had now for weeks: "A dead weight," as he expresses it, "like lead. The doctors regularly tested the sensation in my body from the waist down, by pricking me with straight pins, but I had never felt a thing."

On this day which was to prove the most momentous of their lives, Laura had been fasting over an unusually long period of time. She and many of their friends, also fasting, were following their usual custom of kneeling in prayer for Richard as they listened to the broadcast.

And at 10:55 A.M. it happened. With one of the doctors standing at his bedside, the resurrection power of God took hold of Richard's paralyzed body, and life began to flow into his limbs and organs.

"I felt the power of God go through my whole body," says Richard in recollection. "I began to shake violently and uncontrollably. I suppose this lasted for four or five minutes. Then it stopped, and almost immediately I began to have sensation in my legs.

"The next day," Richard went on, "I was struck again by the power at exactly the same time—10:55 in the morning.

"But you know," he smiled, "I didn't *really* know what had happened. You see, I had never been to a healing service, and it was not until I started to regularly attend Miss Kuhlman's meetings after my healing, that I realized I had experienced the power of God in my own body."

Within an extraordinarily short time after this, Richard was out of the hospital, and in September he returned to school as a high school senior.

Everything that medical science and physiotherapy could do had been employed; but what no human knowledge and skill could accomplish, the Creator of this boy could and did.

The most skillful doctors, physiotherapists and nurses had done their utmost, painstakingly and lovingly, but the doctors were to refer to Richard Kichline as "the patient who has been healed by a higher power."

Richard's total healing was not instantaneous, but when he left the hospital, having learned again to walk with the aid of a walker, many who had been familiar with his condition acknowledged that God is still on his throne, and the age of miracles is not past.

When the Rev. and Mrs. Kichline thanked the doctors at Presbyterian Hospital for their splendid efforts on behalf of their son, the physicians answered in swift response: "Don't thank us. Thank God. He did it." And the Kichlines, of all people, knew how true these words were.

"The wonder of it all continues to grow and grow," says Mrs. Kichline—"that God in His infinite concern, could care so much as to send His healing power from heaven to meet our desperate needs."

In appreciation of His compassion, a small group of committed Christians of various denominations assemble each Wednesday evening in Pastor Kichline's church, to praise God and offer prayer for all who send in their requests for any need whatsoever.

During the years since Richard's healing, God has graciously answered the earnest prayers of this band of consecrated Christians, by bringing untold blessings to many in ways too numerous to recount.

And many who have come to these meetings have found the Lord Jesus Christ as their own personal Saviour. This remains, of course, the greatest of all miracles.

Richard is a living testimony to the power of God. "Because of his healing," states Laura, "people have come from other states, near and far, to attend Kathryn Kuhlman's remarkable services. Here they learn first-hand what God *can* and *does* do."

Twelve and a half years have now passed since Richard Kichline was healed. The sixteen-year-old boy has become a man of twenty-nine. He is over six feet tall and physically strong. He is no less strong in his devotion and sense of dedication to God. He works now at Hillgreen-Lane Organ Company in Alliance, Ohio, building pipe organs, with whose music the Lord's Name shall be praised in many churches.

O for a thousand tongues to sing, My great
    Redeemer's praise;
The glories of my God and King, The triumphs
    of his grace.
Hear Him, ye deaf; His praise, ye dumb, Your
    loosened tongues employ;
Ye blind, behold your Saviour come; And leap,
    ye lame for joy.

CHARLES WESLEY

18

The Dolans
A Little Girl Prayed

The stamp was upside down. The printing—that of a very young child—was done in pencil. All that was on the envelope was: The Preacher Lady, Pittsburgh.

I knew immediately that no child's mother would have permitted the letter to go through the mail had she seen the envelope.

The note inside had been written by a little girl, and was short and to the point. She asked that I please pray that God would make her daddy and mommy not drink, and then she invited me to their home for Christmas. The letter was signed Audrey—and that's all there was EXCEPT the postscript which read: "I forgot to tell you where we live. You get off the bus, and our house is the third big white house from the corner."

I was so amused by both the letter and the envelope that

I read it on my radio broadcast, describing the envelope and the child's printing effort. As I read the entire note, including the postscript, I little knew that Ann Dolan, the child's mother, happened at that exact time to be listening at home to her radio.

As she told me later, she was shocked speechless as she heard the words of the postscript come over the air: "You get off the bus, and our house is the third big white house on the corner."

Ann remembered now, how two days before, her young daughter had been struggling with the dictionary, and then in desperation had innocently asked her mother how to spell PREACHER LADY.

"Why do you want to know?" her mother asked.

"Oh, just 'cause," had come the reply.

Panic-stricken, Ann rushed to Audrey's school to meet the child at dismissal time. As Audrey emerged, her mother confronted her with the question uppermost in her mind, "Did you invite Miss Kuhlman to our house for Christmas?" The child never flinched. Looking her mother straight in the eye, she replied: "Yes."

Half hysterically, her mother asked: "What on earth do you expect to do with her when she comes?"

In firm tones came the answer: "Play with her, of course!"

In that precious little child's mind, there was something far deeper than just wanting to play with the Preacher Lady; what that little girl really wanted MOST was a Christmas mama and daddy. Oh, she loved grandma—she loved her deeply, as deeply as any little girl could possibly love her grandmother. But somehow, no matter how wonderful the grandmother is, she can never take the place of a mother and daddy.

Little Audrey had been largely raised by her grandmother, for her mother had been busy with other things, her social life took so much of her time, she was just too busy to take care of a little girl. Besides, what can you do with a little girl in a cocktail lounge?

Then there was her daddy—of course he loved little Audrey, loved her dearly, but you just don't take little girls to the Sportsman's Club, and what can you do with a little girl when her mother and daddy aren't home most of the time?

Then came the day Audrey heard me make the announcement over the radio that the Thanksgiving Service was to be held at Syria Mosque. With her hopes high, she asked her mother to take her. Ann had never heard of Kathryn Kuhlman, and could not have cared less, but finally, to placate the child, she agreed to take her.

Audrey was sick before Thanksgiving. Leaving the child with her grandmother, Ann was gone from home for three days. But in her heart she loved her little girl: she had left her sick, and had made her a promise which, for a reason she could not fathom, seemed to mean a lot to the child—so she returned home early Thanksgiving morning in time to take Audrey to the service.

Nothing happened. As Ann expressed it in her own words: "Apparently I wasn't touched. I thought the whole thing was silly. My idea of life was to live it up—to have fun. I had spent twenty years of my life in the same crowd, and this was their idea too. But in view of what happened later," she continued, "I think that that afternoon I came under conviction, although I certainly didn't know it at the time."

Then came the Christmas season—the letter with the stamp upside down—the invitation to the big white house, the third from the corner.

When I did not make an appearance at the "big white house" for Christmas, Audrey repeatedly begged her mother to take her to the New Year's Eve Candlelight Service. For several days the child's plea fell on totally deaf ears. Spend New Year's eve in a *religious* service? Not a chance! "Besides," recalled Ann, "I had a big engagement in New York at the Stork Club for that night. I had made the date the preceding August, and I had no intention of disappointing these people at their big New Year's Eve party. I had already sent my clothes on to New York. Nothing was going to stop me.

"And then," she continued, "Audrey asked me again for at least the twentieth time, and to this day I do not know what happened—it certainly must have been the Lord working, for all of a sudden I called New York and cancelled my long-standing reservations, and instead, made reservations on one of the chartered buses going to the New Year's Eve Candlelight Service."

With a smile, Ann continued almost triumphantly, "I dare say, my reservation was the only cancellation at the Stork Club that New Year's Eve."

The weather was very bad that New Year's Eve afternoon. It was snowing hard; the streets were icy and many people were already snowbound. The taxi was unable to make it up the hill to the Dolans' house, so Ann trudged down the hill in the snow with seven-year-old Audrey scuffing ecstatically beside her; her little heart pounding harder than it had ever pounded before, and her little body vibrating with enthusiasm and expectation. They got to the bus just in time.

This New Year's Eve was assuredly different from any other that Ann had ever spent. It was to prove the most momentous of her life, for that night she gave her heart to the Lord and her life was forever changed.

"I wish I could stand on the highest mountain and proclaim to the whole world, the glorious experience of being born again." Ann exclaimed with tears of joy welling up in her dark eyes. "But it is something that one must experience, and it is not something you can fully explain to another. One thing I know, He gives a new life, through the new birth."

Christ did not explain the "how" to Nicodemus. The process is a mystery as seen in John 3:8: "The wind bloweth where it listeth, and thou hearest the sound thereof, but canst not tell whence it cometh, and whither it goeth; so is everyone that is born of the Spirit." Though its causes are hidden, its effects are manifest. The Lord works mysteriously, but His results are definite.

"I, if I be lifted up from the earth, will draw all men unto myself." And when, bound to His cross, He is lifted up before men's eyes, by some strange power which defies analysis, dying He brings them life; bound He brings them liberty; suffering He redeems them from the greatest anguish the soul can know, the agony of hopeless despair; and everlastingly loving he challenges them, and claims them, and will never let them go until He makes them His forever.

When little Audrey's daddy, Red Dolan, came in from a party at his club at around 8 A.M., he brought trinkets and noisemakers for his young daughter—the sort of thing that had always thrilled her before. But Audrey didn't care about any noisemakers on this day. It was as if she had already gotten what she wanted from the Lord.

But it was to be another year before she got all she wanted from Him, for it took that long for her father to accept Christ. However, during that year, another member of the Dolan family was to be marvelously touched and healed by the power of God—*grandpa!*

Ann's father had been a drunkard for sixty years—"I never remember my dad sober" said Ann.

He was a musician and would often stay away from home three or four weeks at a time. Upon coming home, he would frequently be so sick that he would lie out on the lawn in front of the house, unable to move. After each such time it seemed to take longer to sober him up.

Before Ann and Red were married, Red had tried to remedy the situation, but grandpa could not or would not change his ways. Every doctor in Carnegie, Pennsylvania, now knew him, loved him and tried to help him. Their verdict was unanimous: something had to be done for grandpa!

A few months after Ann's conversion, grandpa engaged in what was to prove his last bout with liquor.

He had been drinking heavily for weeks. The last time anyone had seen him, he looked the typical "bum"—one boot over one shoe; no shoelaces; someone's filthy cap on his head, and he had lost his glasses so he couldn't see. He was by now so drunk that his trousers wouldn't stay up, and he had taken an old piece of rope to hold them in place. Grandma, looking for him, came down and said to Ann, "I think dad's just about done. I haven't seen him for five whole days. He was so miserable when he left the house, I'm afraid he may have done away with himself. He hasn't eaten for days—just drinking all the time."

This was a Saturday night, and Ann replied, "I will be going to Miss Kuhlman's service tomorrow. Don't worry, mother, we'll pray for dad. You just stay home and pray for him, too."

The next night—and the next—dad still hadn't come home. The third night Ann's mother came down and said: "I think dad is in the barn."

They searched carefully all over the barn, but could find no trace of grandpa. As it was by now after 9 o'clock at night, Ann and Audrey started home, praying along the way. Suddenly Audrey said, "I hear something coming down the road."

Ann recognized the sound of her father's footsteps— that curious dragging sound which meant he was too weak to pick up his feet. And then he appeared around the bend of the road.

Grandpa didn't seem to know either his daughter or granddaughter, but Audrey went over to him there in the middle of the road, and said, "Grandpa, I love you; and you don't know how much Jesus loves you."

The man was so sick he couldn't stand. All he wanted was money for a drink.

Then Ann said: "Dad—just let's kneel down here." They all knelt together on the side of the road and Ann prayed very simply, "Lord, take him. Whatever way you want him, just take him."

In that instant, grandpa got up from his knees, walked straight up the hill with amazing strength, entered the house, took off his clothes, and bathed and shaved.

Christ had come into his heart, and grandpa was a new creature in Christ Jesus—"Old things having passed away, and behold, all things had become new!"

Two days later found grandpa at the service at Carnegie Hall, publicly acknowledging Christ as his Saviour. He was never again to take—or even want—another drink.

Meanwhile Red Dolan was fighting his own convictions. Months had passed now since Ann's, and then her father's, conversion. Red thought it a wonderful thing that his wife had given her heart to the Lord. Wonderful for her, that is, but this sort of thing was definitely not for him.

God always hears little girls' prayers!

And then it happened. One day, standing at the end of a bar, having ordered his drink but never having touched it, something happened to Red Dolan that to this hour he cannot fully explain, and yet it was the most powerful force that had ever seized his person.

He suddenly saw himself as God saw him, a sinner—wretched—a miserable offender against God; a man not worthy of a precious little girl's pure love; a man who needed to be cleansed from all unrighteousness, and needing to be delivered from the power of sin.

Involuntarily he dropped to his knees at the end of the bar—and in a barroom filled with men, he cried out unashamedly: "God be merciful to me, a sinner."

That was all—it was a short prayer—but it came from a sincere and penitent heart; it came from the heart of a man who was sick of sin; a man who wanted to be freed from the power of sin; a man who wanted the reality of Christ in his life—the experience that his little girl had and the reality of the person of Jesus, as reflected in the life of Ann. He had seen what that experience had done in the life of grandpa, and he knew it was real!

He swears there was no more to his prayer than that—but in that moment, the greatest miracle a human being can know, took place. Red became a new creature in Christ Jesus, and was instantly, completely and permanently delivered from liquor.

The Dolans have a new home—a Christian home—which they enjoy *together*. Audrey has new parents—their lives dedicated to Christ. With two years as a student at Carnegie Institute of Technology, Audrey's faith is as secure, as solid, as sound and as simple as when she put the stamp on the envelope upside down, and wrote her first letter to her *Preacher Lady*.

THIS IS GOD; that in the balcony of an auditorium, a woman gave herself to the Lord, that at the end of a country road, her father accepted Him; that in a crowded bar, her husband gave Him his heart. And all because a little girl prayed—for Jesus' sake.

19

James McCutcheon
"Truly a Miracle!"

Holding up the X-rays and pointing with his pencil, he exclaimed: "A miracle—that's all I can call it! In all my years of practice I've never seen anything like this—a piece of bone has grown where there was none before. This bone is supporting your weight, and *that's* why you can walk."

The speaker was the long-time personal physician of James McCutcheon.

A few days earlier Jim had stopped by his office for a flu shot. As a personal favor, the doctor had asked Jim to have these X-rays made—at his expense. Why? Because his scientific curiosity had gotten the better of him. Familiar with Jim's medical history; having carefully studied the previous series of X-rays made before and after Jim's five unsuccessful operations to correct a broken hip, the doctor knew there existed a bone separation which made it medically impossible for Jim to walk. How and why, then, *was* he walking? This is what the physician had to know.

When the accident had occurred, Jim was working as head mechanic on a construction job at Lorain, Ohio. They were putting in a railroad yard for an ore dock, and Jim at the time was breaking in a new man on the bulldozer.

It was four o'clock on a late October afternoon—time to park the equipment. Jim stood on a railroad cross-tie, signaling in the driver, and either the inexperienced driver did not see the signal or he misinterpreted it, for he made a wrong turn. The bulldozer struck the timber on which Jim was standing. It flew up, striking him on the leg, and tossing him ten feet in the air. He landed hard on the ground on his right hip, and whether the blow from the timber did the damage—or the force of the heavy fall of a 210-pound man—no one knows.

"I've never been knocked out in my life," Jim says with a grin, and he wasn't knocked unconscious now. He got up, grabbed a short shovel from a close-by laborer, and using it as a cane, he walked about ten feet, and then fell down. This time, he could not get up, and they took him on a stretcher to St. Joseph's Hospital in Lorain. There they discovered that the ball of his hip was broken off square and clean, "just as if you had taken a hack-saw and cut it off."

Two days later he was put in a cast, and six days later, on November 6, 1947, the first of the five operations—each seeming more painful than the last—was performed.

A threaded wood screw made of cadmium, steel and silver, four and a half inches long and five-sixteenths of an inch in diameter, was inserted in the upper femur (thigh bone) through the broken hip ball.

Jim was in the hospital for six pain-filled weeks. He then returned to Pittsburgh, and after several weeks of unabated pain, went to his own doctor for examination.

X-rays were taken which revealed that the screw in his hip was too long, and the end was protruding from the ball into the socket. Hence, every time he moved his leg, the screw dug deep into the socket. Further, the pictures showed that the fragments of the bone had not been brought together: there was a clearly discernible separation between the femur and the ball of the hip, and decalcification had already set in in the broken ball.

January 19, 1948, was the McCutcheons' twenty-fifth wedding anniversary. Jim celebrated it by going into Columbia Hospital in Pittsburgh for his second operation, where a shorter screw was inserted.

Still unable to walk after surgery, X-rays showed that *this screw* had missed the broken ball. Three weeks later, a third operation was performed and a third screw inserted. This, too, failed to bring the broken fragments of the bone into proper relation, one with the other.

Jim's fourth operation in March, 1948, consisted of removing the third screw which had already started to work loose, and putting the patient in a so-called "spike" cast, which encased the entire body except for his two arms and one leg. This was intended to remain on for ten weeks, but it buckled after a few days, and the doctors removed it.

Jim still could not walk. He was in continual, intense pain and was greatly worried about when and if he would ever be able to go back to work.

The doctors by now vouchsafed that according to his last X-rays, he *should* be able to get around better than he was doing.

But it was Jim's hip, and he knew he simply could not stand on his right leg—it would bear no weight whatsoever. It seemed all too obvious to Jim that what had been wrong from the beginning was *still* wrong.

It suddenly occurred to him that the last X-rays had been taken only while he was in a prone position. He called this to the attention of his doctor, and asked that more pictures be taken while he was standing upright. This was done, and Jim was proved right: when he stood, the same separation was clearly visible; there was still no connection between the upper part of the thigh bone and the hip socket.

In August of 1948, he was to undergo what proved his last operation—this time in Allegheny General Hospital in Pittsburgh. The doctor this time, instead of reopening the old incision on the side of his hip, made a new incision across the front of his hip. A piece of bone was cut from the upper femur, and laid directly over the break—being secured with a nail.

Jim was then put once more into a "spike" cast for ten weeks, and this time it *remained* for ten weeks. At the end of it all, this bone-grafting operation proved unsuccessful, because of the decalcification. The bone simply would not knit.

By this time Jim was desperate. Ten months of ceaseless, severe pain; five operations, and he was not only no better but worse than before the first surgery had been performed, because of the progressive decalcification.

It was while visiting her husband as he lay in Allegheny

General Hospital, that Alma's attention had been drawn to the services. Each day on her way to the hospital she passed Carnegie Hall in the streetcar, and saw the crowds and heard the singing.

Her curiosity was aroused and she stopped in the auditorium one day on the way to the hospital. Already a committed Christian and a woman of great faith, she knew what it was all about. Subsequently she sent in several prayer requests, unknown to Jim for as he says, "I belonged to a church, but I wasn't much of a Christian, and Alma knew I didn't believe in divine healing."

The doctors had told Jim now that his only hope lay in entirely replacing the broken hip ball with an artificial one of plastic and silver.

This sixth operation had already been scheduled, when Alma's sister, in whose house the McCutcheons were then living, joined with Alma in pleading with Jim to go to a service. Jim assented in a half-hearted manner. "One of these days we'll go," he promised.

But as he thought the matter over, he decided if he were going at all he had better go soon—before it was time to enter the hospital for his next operation.

"I was so discouraged with all the pain and the prospects of still another operation which might well fail, as had all those in the past, that I was willing to try anything—even one of these services," he says with a smile.

And thus the next week he went to his first service at Carnegie Hall—alone.

Unable to stand even two minutes without support, he was now using a heavy cane instead of the more cumbersome crutches, but even with this aid, being on his feet for any period of time caused him acute discomfort. This day he stood for three hours waiting for the doors to open, and when he finally got inside the hall, he found all the seats taken. By now exhausted, discouraged and in great pain, he went back home and told his wife what had happened.

The next week his sister-in-law offered to take him and he accepted her offer. This time to be safe, they went armed with folding chairs.

"I went in the doors with a big heavy cane in one hand and the folding chair in the other," recalls Jim, "and the first thing I knew I was sitting on the platform. How I got there, I'll never know. I must have been just carried and pushed along with the crowd."

Jim had been a heavy smoker for thirty-five years, and before the service started he went down to the men's lounge to smoke a cigarette. He cannot tell you exactly why, but after the service he was to lay his pack of cigarettes down and he has never smoked again.

"That was a curious thing," he says, "because Miss Kuhlman never said one word about smoking, one way or the other."

Jim actually didn't know what to think of the service. He had never seen anything like it before, and he watched, purely as a spectator, understanding very little of what it was all about.

His eldest married daughter, who had been listening regularly to the broadcasts, was particularly eager to go to Carnegie Hall to a service, so the following week he went with her while Alma babysat with the children.

They got seats this time midway back in the hall. Suddenly in the midst of the service, "a great heat came over me," Jim says. "It felt as if there were a fire under my chair, and the sweat just poured off me."

His daughter had her hand on his knee, and she says in recollection, "Waves of electricity seemed to go from his leg into my arm."

The first thing Jim knew, and to his utter amazement, his cane was stashed under the seat and he was up on his feet and out in the aisle, his daughter beside him. Without a moment's hesitation or doubt or fear, he walked, unaided down the aisle to the platform. Without hesitation, he climbed the high steps to the platform.

"When I got up there," he says, "Miss Kuhlman told me to lift my leg high and stamp my foot. I did, and I've been doing it ever since!"

This was November 5, 1949. From that day to this, he has never used a cane, or had any trouble whatsoever with his hip or leg. He can run and jump, and demonstrate the strength of his right leg by standing on it one-legged, so that it bears the full weight of his over two hundred pounds. The only evidence that there was ever anything wrong, lies in the fact that he walks with a slight limp.

He gave his heart to the Lord that day in 1949, and he has brought many to Christ by his witness—among the first, his own nephew.

When he got home that evening, he was still almost incredulous at what had happened. His wife was less surprised—for she had long known the power of God to heal—but no less joyful. The family was called together in celebration and thanksgiving. A gala feast was prepared, for the hunting season had just opened, and Jim's son-in-law had just come home laden with small game.

Jim's nephew was, of all of them, perhaps the most aghast at what had happened: aghast not only to see Jim *walk,* but at the instantaneous restoration of muscle in the long unused leg.

He kept feeling it, and saying, "Just look at the muscle you've suddenly developed."

Often during the next weeks he would go down to the first floor to his uncle's apartment, and with a puzzled expression on his face, feel Jim's leg. Through the wonder of his healing, he was to give his heart to Jesus before too long a time had passed.

Jim immediately went to work for an auto-repair company until 1956, at which time he went to work for the company he had worked for at the time of his accident. The company later went out of business, and he went back to auto repairing again. He is still working as a mechanic.

"I do hard work," he says. "There are very few of my age who can work as I do, and after working eight hours a day at the garage, I go home and do heavy work there. Last thing I did, for instance, was to put cement steps in the back, and I did all the excavation myself."

Jim works five days a week, but one day on which he does *not* work is Friday. That is the day of the Miracle Service—the day of the week on which he was healed. Every Friday, come what may, Jim ushers at the services at Carnegie Hall.

From his healing in 1949 until 1960, Jim never bothered to go back to his doctor for more X-rays. "I knew I was healed, that was good enough for me. I didn't need it confirmed," he says.

But knowing that unbelievers demand scientific proof, he procured a full set of X-rays showing before and after pictures of each operation. It was not until 1960, when he went for the flu shot, that he subsequently obtained the final pictures, showing the piece of new bone which had grown completely over the cleavage between the ball of the hip and the upper thigh bone, thus welding the formerly separated fragments into one strong, solid piece of bone. This is the bone which now, and apparently from the moment of his healing, has carried his weight.

"The Lord had to put it there," says Jim, "there was no other way." And with this, his surgeon emphatically agrees. "This is truly a miracle," were his words.

Jim, a great, rugged, husky man, takes obvious pride in the fact that nothing, not even the fall he took in the accident, has ever knocked him out.

"But that isn't quite true," he says now with a smile. "What I should have said is that I've never been knocked out in my life except by the power of the Lord!"

20

The Crider Case
"Please Let Him Walk!"

The mother stood holding the little club-footed baby in her arms, contemplating suicide. She knew exactly how she was going to do it: she would throw her baby and herself under a fast-moving streetcar. She felt she could not have her child go through life as a cripple. She had seen so many deformed, helpless children that the very thought of her own child going through life in that condition was more than she could bear.

Ever since Jean could remember, she had wanted children, and hoped to have both a boy and a girl. After Nancy had been born six years before, Jean then prayed that she would soon have a son. Five years later when she found herself pregnant again, she offered a spontaneous prayer, "O Lord, let it be a boy!"

When the time came for her delivery, this prayer was

still on her lips and in her heart, and it seemed that her cup of happiness was full, when just coming out of the ether, she heard her husband say, "You have your little boy, honey." And then—

Only a mother can fully understand what were the feelings, the emotions, the shock to both mind and body, when with all the depth of loss that he had in his being—with all the tenderness that any man has ever felt; with his own spirit so crushed that he could scarcely speak, Elmer Crider took his wife's hand and gently told her the truth. There was something dreadfully wrong with one of the baby's feet.

When the nurse came into Jean's room a few minutes later, she took in the situation at a glance, "You told her?" she said to Elmer. At his nod, she left the room, and shortly thereafter, the doctor himself brought the baby in to the patient.

"I pulled the receiving blanket back," recalls Jean, "and I looked at his little foot, and I just wanted to die. 'Why, O Lord,' I asked, 'couldn't it have been me instead?' "

The baby's tiny foot was turned back until his toes touched his heel, and where there should have been bone, there was only flesh.

"What can you do for it?" was Jean's first agonized question.

"We will have to put him in a brace," he said.

"Will he ever be able to walk, will he be all right?" Jean demanded.

"Well—" responded the doctor, "We'll have to see. A thing like this takes time, you know."

Two days later they put the brace on the baby. "He looked so pitiful," Jean says, "I cried when I looked at him. I just didn't know what to do. 'Bring him back to see me when he's four weeks old,' the doctor told me—'and we'll see then how things are.' "

When Jean left the hospital with little Ronnie, she did not go home rejoicing over a perfect little son. She went home as a heartbroken mother of a probably hopeless cripple.

In three weeks Elmer took the baby back to the doctor, who was still noncommital.

When Ronnie was five weeks old, his mother took him back for a third visit. The doctor removed the brace which the baby had by now outgrown. "Leave it off," he said, "until at about six months old he begins to pull himself up in his crib."

The contrast between the two little legs was pathetic to see—the one so chubby and strong; the other so pitifully thin and by now so weak.

Jean was carefully instructed by the doctor as to the physiotherapy to use, and she assiduously massaged the little leg and foot at home, but with little effect, for still there was nothing but flesh where bone was supposed to be, and the foot still turned back.

"Be careful," warned the doctor. "Don't let him put any pressure on his leg whatsoever. Don't let him push against you, or against his buggy or crib, for the foot will snap back."

Ronnie was already extremely active, and all Jean could think was, "What am I going to do with him to make *sure* no pressure is ever exerted on this foot?"

Ronnie was a gorgeous baby—responsive, robust and unusually good-looking, with a completely captivating smile. Cooing and gurgling at everyone he saw, strangers repeatedly came up to Jean whenever she had him out, to talk to Ronnie, and then to compliment his mother on her beautiful child. Jean would always smile, but her eyes would dart to the blankets which invariably covered his crippled leg. She would smile, and her heart would break.

The memory of the last time she took Ronnie to the doctor will forever remain with Jean.

By now Ronnie was five months old. In addition to the club foot, the little leg itself was considerably shorter than the other normal one.

"When he begins to pull himself up," the doctor had said that day, "we will go into the matter of surgery. The operation will involve his hip and his foot. One leg will inevitably be shorter than the other, but at least he will be able to *walk*."

Jean looked at the beautiful baby lying on the examining table. Walk? Yes, perhaps, but never to run, never to play football or baseball, never to be like other children.

"No one will ever know how I felt that day," confided Jean. "When I left the Jenkins Arcade Building holding Ronnie in my arms, I wanted more than anything in the world to protect him. I felt so helpless. I could see him going through life as a cripple—hurt and bewildered when his friends made fun of him. And I knew I was powerless to save him from all this."

That was the day when Jean planned to throw herself and him in front of a streetcar. The only thing that prevented her from doing this was the thought of her six-year-old Nancy at home. What would become of her? Who would take care of *her* without a mother?

"I guess this was really God speaking to my heart," Jean says. "*He* stopped my doing what I thought I wanted to do that afternoon."

For years Jean had listened every morning to the Arthur Godfrey program as she went about her work, but for some extraordinary reason that she couldn't then understand (although she does now) the morning after her visit to the doctor she changed the station on her radio and "Suddenly," she recalls, "I heard a voice: HAVE YOU BEEN WAITING FOR ME? it said."

"I stopped in my tracks, and answered aloud, 'Yes, I have.' The voice I heard was that of Kathryn Kuhlman."

This was the first time Jean had ever heard the broadcast. It was either a Thursday or a Friday, and a service was announced for that afternoon. She didn't stop to think twice. Getting Nancy ready and bundling Ronnie up, being especially careful as always that the blankets covering his legs were well secured so that they could not work loose, they all left for Carnegie Hall. They sat in a corner of the balcony surrounded by people such as, Jean says now, she had never known existed—people at the service who are there not only because they seek help for themselves, but also there because they want to share one another's burdens.

"Everyone made a big fuss over Ronnie," she says, "and all I could think was, 'if only they could see his foot and leg.'"

Jean went home inspired and elated over what she had seen and felt at Carnegie Auditorium that afternoon. She was indescribably thrilled over having witnessed something that was entirely new to her: the power of God in action.

When Elmer came home from work that evening, Jean met him at the door, bubbling over with happiness and hope. Her husband hadn't seen her that way since little Ronnie had been born.

She told him of the service, and asked his permission to write out a prayer request for their little son's healing. Elmer's response was instantaneous: "Sure—go ahead," he said—"Let's do it together right now!"

So they sat down together and wrote out the request. They had never done such a thing before, and were not quite sure of the proper way to do it. But when they had finished, they felt impelled to kneel together and pray over it, asking God for help.

Immediately afterward, Elmer went out with the letter and mailed it.

From that time on, every morning found Jean on her knees throughout the broadcast. She would kneel beside Ronnie, holding in her hands his little crippled leg and twisted foot, "And each time," Jean says, "I could feel his leg and foot twitch and jump as the power of God actually went through them."

Jean says she learned things she had never known before as she listened.

She had attended Sunday school, and even taught Sunday school, but she had never been really aware of her own sins before. Now as she listened to the broadcast each morning, she knew that she had to have her sins forgiven.

"One day, right in the kitchen at home," said Jean, "I knelt and confessed all my sins to God. Little by little, I was to give up drinking and smoking. I gave my life over to God, and told Him anything He wanted of me I would do. I vowed to give Him the praise and all the glory, whatever happened."

Ronnie kept getting better and better. When he was

about a year old, he could stand, but his leg still turned out. Jean continued to pray, confident that his healing would soon be complete. However, as she prayed, her eyes constantly strayed to Ronnie's crippled leg, as if waiting to see the miracle take place.

It was Elmer who, with remarkable insight, said to her, "Maybe you're going about this the wrong way. Perhaps you should stop *looking* at his leg all the time you're praying. You act as if you're questioning God's promise to heal; as if you're *challenging* Him to hurry up; as if maybe you're afraid He won't. It seems to me you should think and *believe* that the leg is already healed. You know," he continued, "the Bible says WHAT THINGS SOEVER YE DESIRE, WHEN YE PRAY, BELIEVE THAT YE RECEIVE THEM, AND YE SHALL HAVE THEM" (Mark 11:24).

Elmer had unknowingly discovered, and expressed to his wife, two basic precepts of divine healing: *believe* that it is already done, even as you pray, and focus your attention not on the ailment, but on Jesus Christ.

Jean listened to her husband, and as she says, "I saw then that he was right, so I just gave it to God and prayed, 'O God, please take the *fear* from me that the leg *isn't* healed.' "

The next day during the broadcast, Jean listened intently to every word that I had to say during my little heart-to-heart talk, and surely I was led of the Holy Spirit to speak to that precious mother, for over and over I emphasized the fact that fear was one of the greatest enemies that an individual could take into his life. I stressed the fact that we lose our fear by fastening our attention, not on the thing to be feared, or on the fear of this fear, but on Christ who is our deliverance from fear.

Not knowing that there in the kitchen of her home was a mother who was hanging on every word that I was speaking, I continued, "Take your eyes off of circumstances; take your eyes off of conditions; take your eyes off of the affliction and fix your eyes on Jesus, for at the heart of your faith is a person, the very Son of the living God, whose power is greater than any enemy you face; greater than circumstances; greater than the problems in your life."

In an instant, Jean Crider took her child in her arms and stood him in a corner of the room by himself. On her knees, her eyes on God and not on her baby; her eyes on Christ and not on his poor little club foot, she looked up and prayed: "Oh, Lord—PLEASE LET HIM WALK—please let his first steps be straight and strong."

As she rose from her knees, she looked at Ronnie. Without really thinking, she held out her arms to him. And the miracle came to pass. He walked toward her—perfectly—legs and feet both strong and straight, and those little legs have remained strong and straight to this very day. That, beloved, is the power of God in action—that is the power of God, released in response to unqualified faith.

Ronnie's healing occurred in 1952. The ten-year-old boy is today absolutely perfect, and the fastest runner in his class at school. When asked recently what he wanted to be when he grew to be a man, he quickly replied, "An usher at the Kathryn Kuhlman services!" Right there on the spot I promised him a job as soon as he was old enough!

In all my experience I do not ever remember a child who

was more conscious of the mercy of God in his healing; a youngster with a greater understanding of the spiritual truths; none more deeply grateful for two good legs and two good feet. It is as though God had anointed this child with a very definite insight into spiritual things when in His tender mercy, He straightened the little club foot.

The Crider family had known little of the things of God when Ronnie was born. They know now, and are living the lives of thoroughly committed Christians, whose first thought is always of God, and whose primary ambition is to glorify Him in their lives.

They have learned that there is a POWER that man can wield when mortal aid is vain—that there is a love that never fails when human strength gives way: that power is PRAYER through Jesus Christ the Lord, and that LOVE is God Himself, the Hand that moves the world to help a soul, alone.

21

Harry Stephenson
Hot Dogs and Onions!

"Hot dogs and onions, and I *never* tasted anything so good in all my life!"

I turned to the man and said, "Do you mean to tell me that not having had anything whatsoever to eat for thirty days, and not even able to take water, that you ate *hot dogs* and *onions*? That's enough to kill a *well* person!"

"Yes, ma'am. I ate three hot dogs and everything that went with 'em. I was hungry and had a lot of space to fill.

"I remember how my wife looked at me and said, 'I don't know how in the world you can do it after all you have gone through. I know for sure, now, that the Lord has really healed you.' "

Those words came from Harry Stephenson, who had been sent home from the hospital to die of cancer of the bowels and stomach. The lining of his stomach had been completely eaten out by the malignancy.

In the beginning his trouble had been diagnosed as a nervous ulcerated stomach. Every possible treatment was given to correct the condition, but it continued to grow worse, and as his physical discomfort increased and he grew weaker, it became more and more difficult to continue on his strenuous job as a steamfitter at the steel works.

Harry's illness had been a lengthy one. A valued and longtime employee of Carnegie Steel Company in Duquesne, Pennsylvania, he had for eleven years spent most of his time off in doctor's offices. No one could say he lacked for good medical care, as in all, over the years, some twenty-eight doctors had been consulted.

Finally, five years after the onset of the sickness which no amount of medical treatment had thus far helped, his doctor urged hospitalization. He filled out the necessary papers, and Harry was admitted to the Veterans Administration Hospital in Aspinwall, Pennsylvania. After extensive laboratory tests, new treatment and medication were administered in an attempt to form a lining for his stomach, for by now the natural lining had become completely eroded.

After the doctors had done everything scientifically possible, Harry was released from the hospital no better than when he had entered, and over the next three years, his health declined with alarming rapidity. In shocking condition, he was hospitalized for the second time.

Harry Stephenson was now a wraith—a mere shadow of his former self. He had once been a big, strapping man, weighing in the vicinity of 190 pounds. Now he weighed only 114 pounds.

He was in continual severe pain in spite of the pain-killing drugs he was taking. For some time his only nourishment had been an occasional glass of goat's milk. Now he could not retain even water on his stomach, and the liquid necessary to sustain life he obtained by sucking ice.

Extensive laboratory tests were once more conducted, including the examination of tissue specimens. At last, on the basis of these tests, a firm diagnosis was finally made, and the news was as bad as it could possibly be: inoperable cancer of the stomach and bowels.

The ten doctors on the board of the Veterans Administration Hospital* pulled no punches. They told Harry precisely what the situation was: that they had done all for him that was medically possible to do for any human being, but in their opinion his condition was hopeless. They suggested that he might go to the cancer hospital in New York in the admittedly forlorn hope that something could be done for him there.

He was thus discharged from the Pennsylvania hospital, given by the doctors approximately a month to live. Too sick to travel, and with complete confidence in the doctors who had cared for him in Aspinwall, he did not even consider the New York trip. If he were going to die, he wanted to die at home.

Each day of the next three weeks seemed more tortuous than the last. The pain had become excruciating, and was now impervious to the increasingly large doses of morphine he was taking. The odor characteristic of some terminal cancers had become so nauseating that Harry was unable, not only to sleep in the same bedroom with his wife, but even on the same floor with other members of

*His records are at this hospital.

his family. He was obliged to sleep on an army cot loaned by a friend which was placed downstairs at the far end of the house.

The Stephenson family was desperate. Their daughter, Audrey, who had been saved at an early age, had been praying desperately for her father's salvation and healing.

On that last Wednesday, Harry was in worse shape than he had ever been before. He was screaming like an animal with pain that no drug could alleviate. His frightened wife tried in vain to reach the V.A. hospital. She knew that they were better equipped there to help him than was she at home. But she was unable to reach the hospital.

"We realize now," says Harry, "that it was the Holy Spirit Himself who kept that call from being completed, for it was that very day that a friend of ours who is a nurse and knew all along that I had cancer, dropped in to visit us."

It was this nurse who told the Stephensons about Kathryn Kuhlman's services and the power of God to heal.

"Why don't you send a telegram to her, Mildred," she asked Mrs. Stephenson, "and request her to pray for Harry!"

The Stephensons had never heard the radio broadcasts; had never attended a service; indeed, they had never even heard the name of Kathryn Kuhlman before this. They were frankly skeptical.

"Well," said the nurse, "you've tried everything else, and nothing can help Harry now in the way of medical treatment. Why don't you try this?"

The next day—Thursday—the telegram was sent.

"Friday," says Harry, his face radiant in recollection, "turned out to be the most blessed day of my life. This was the day of my rebirth, my life in Christ, and the promise of life eternal."

The pain that morning was almost intolerable. He was lying on the couch on the sunporch, listening to the radio. Mildred was in the kitchen, and Audrey was upstairs praying for him.

"Then," he recalls, "over the air I heard the voice of Kathryn Kuhlman call me by name in earnest prayer."

Scarcely aware of what he was doing, Harry began to pray along with her: "Dear Lord, have mercy on me. Forgive me all that I have done wrong all my life." In an unconscious gesture of supplication, he put out his hand, and implored, "Let me be one of those you touch today."

"Suddenly the power of the Holy Spirit came upon me, and the pain left instantly and completely," recalls Harry. "And I began to shake and sob and cry out. My wife and daughter didn't know about the working of the Holy Spirit and I scared them half to death!"

They both believed that Harry Stephenson was dying. His daughter, now a schoolteacher, went up to her bedroom and got her Bible and started to pray. Mildred, in a panic, wanted to get a doctor immediately, but Harry prevented her.

He did not at once identify what was happening to him as the working of the Holy Spirit, for he had never before experienced it. But he *did* know that he no longer had pain and that he was not dying. He felt that something wonderful was happening to him, and it was; he was not only receiving God's healing for his physical body, but a far greater miracle was taking place—the salvation of his soul.

"And then," he said, "I heard Miss Kuhlman say, Eat in the name of Jesus." Harry was flabbergasted. Eat? Eat anything he wanted after his long, gradual starvation, and after thirty days when nothing, not even water, had stayed down?

After his shaking had stopped, and the power had left his body, Harry was to turn to his wife and say, "You know, Mildred, I'm hungry as can be. Please fix me something to eat." In reply to her startled "WHAT?" he said, "Yes, and do you know what I want? Some *fried eggs!*" So fried eggs it was.

Harry was so weak he could hardly walk, but he struggled up from the couch and painstakingly made his way out to the kitchen, where he sat down at the table for the first time in many weeks. He had a cup of tea, a slice of toast, and two fried eggs. They stayed down, and as Harry says with a grin, "I thought I never tasted anything so good in my entire life!"

When that evening at suppertime his wife asked him what he'd like to eat, he replied, "Hot dogs and onions and all the trimmings, and I'm starved! You'd better make me three." She did, and he ate them all.

"If I'd thought the fried eggs were good, those hot dogs were out of this world!" he said with a smile.

Mildred just looked at him in amazement. "*How* are you suddenly able to eat like this?" she asked. Harry's answer was simple:

"Because the Lord touched me," he said.

It was exactly twenty-one days since he had been discharged from the Veterans Administration hospital to die.

The neighbors were amazed by his healing, but there was one person among those who knew Harry who was possibly the most dumbfounded of all.

It was three days after his healing, Harry was out in front of his house washing his car, when one of the doctors who had said he couldn't possibly live more than a month when he left the hospital drove by.

"I couldn't pretend to describe the expression on that man's face when he saw me," Harry grinned. "He got as white as a sheet and stared at me so hard he almost wrecked his car."

The physician brought his car to a halt, got out and came over to Harry. "What on earth has *happened* to you?" he gasped. When Harry told him that it was the work of God, the medical man looked thoughtful, and then he nodded. "Yes," he said, "It had to be, for nothing and no one except God could have helped you."

Harry regained his lost weight—in fact, before too long had passed he weighed 196 pounds, and had to reduce, as he had difficulty in climbing around on his job!

Since his healing, which occurred thirteen years ago, Harry has not, as he puts it, "even had so much as a headache. From that day to this," he says, "I haven't had to have a doctor. The only time I ever see one is when I have to go to the company doctor for an examination at work. Furthermore, from that day to this, I've eaten everything that is put on the table!"

Well known in the valley where he has lived and worked for so long, scores of people personally witnessed the wonder of what might be called this man's resurrection. His very appearance of renewed health and vitality became a living and cogent testimony to the love and power of God.

As Harry says, to be healed when at the brink of death

was a great and glorious thing.

"But even greater," he says, "was the realization that my soul had been saved from sin at the same time my body was healed of cancer. After many years of smoking, drinking, swearing and every other sin possible, I was instantaneously changed—made a new creature in Christ. My only desire from that moment on was to serve Him with all my being." And this he continues to do.

Through his personal witnesses and changed life, he has brought many to Christ, including his entire family.

The story of Harry Stephenson is the story of a miracle. It is ample proof that I, Kathryn Kuhlman, have nothing to do with these healings, for this man had never seen me, and was not even in the auditorium when he was touched by Jesus.

This is the power of God. We cannot analyze God—we can only gratefully accept Him and thankfully receive His marvelous power in our lives—giving Him all praise and glory forever.

In our courts of law, cases of great importance are often decided solely on the basis of testimony. The testimony of a reputable and competent witness is invariably considered, and the courts, knowing its great value, do not hesitate to accept it.

The miracles wrought by Christ and by the power of the Holy Spirit are made credible to us not only by trustworthy testimony; not only by reliable witnesses, but also by unimpeachable circumstantial evidence as contained in detailed medical records.

On what basis, then, rests the assertion that miracles are not credible? Are they not supported by testimony?

Are the witnesses not competent or trustworthy? Is the circumstantial evidence of countless medical records to be negated?

These are miracles of such a kind as to admit proof from both human testimony and circumstantial evidence. They were so public as to command attention, and were of such a nature as to preclude the possibility of delusion and deception.

You will have observed that all the healings recorded in this book date back a number of years. We could have told you of healings which occurred yesterday or last week, but we have chosen to report healings of long standing, for a definite purpose: Namely, to refute any idea that such healings are hysterical in nature and thus do not stand the test of time.

22

George Speedy
Those Whom God Heals, Stay Healed!

It was the Thanksgiving Day Service and I was waiting to go onto the platform, when an usher brought me an orchid, saying that a gentleman had asked him to bring it to me to wear during the service.

I opened the attached card and read: "In appreciation for what you have done for me—'Speedy.' "

Pinning on the flower, I walked onto the platform and announced the first hymn. After the singing I stopped the service, read the card to the congregation, and asked the person who had sent it to come forward.

Down the aisle came a man about forty-years old, with his face beaming. As he stood before me, I said, "Speedy— I dare say this is the first orchid you ever bought in your life." Quickly came the reply: "Not only the first *orchid,* Miss Kuhlman, but the first *flower.* But you know," he continued with a grin, "for months the tavern owners of Warren, Ohio, thought I was in the floral business. You see, I used to work for a vault company, delivering vaults to the cemeteries, and I would take the fresh flowers lying on new graves. Then I'd make the round of the taverns, supplying them with fresh flowers in exchange for my drinks!"

George Speedy didn't start out to be an alcoholic; does anyone, ever?

Like most young people, he drank for kicks and the feeling of confidence it gave him, but he started a little earlier than most. "At the age of eight," he relates, "I would go out to the garage and drain my father's empty whisky bottles—or swipe hard cider from my granddad's barrel."

When Speedy was fourteen, the family moved to Warren, Ohio, where he soon made new friends who, like himself, thought it was great sport to get a bottle of wine or brandy whenever they could.

By the time he was married at twenty, he was well on his way to becoming an alcoholic—often boasting that he could drink most men under the table, but because he was young and strong, with a healthy appetite for good food, no one guessed that he was already on the road to his own destruction.

He and his young wife, Kay, were very much in love, and he worked steadily for quite a while after their marriage, although as she says, "I seldom saw any money. We had only the bare necessities—the rest went for booze."

When payday was every two weeks, things weren't too bad, but then Speedy got a job paying every week—so every five days there were two days lost—payday on which he celebrated, and the day after, on which he sobered up. But in spite of his drinking, George Speedy was an excellent worker at whatever job he held, and because of this, he was given chance after chance by his employer. Basically a good man, always ready to help a friend in need, he bitterly resented any criticism of his drinking, insisting that he was harming no one but himself. He steadfastly refused to see what it was doing to his marriage.

As his wife says: "Our home life became a hell on earth before it was over. Speedy would come home drunk night after night, mean and quarrelsome, and the children became so afraid of him they remarked more than once that they wished he would never come home at all."

His money was now gone long before payday, for the weekend binges were no longer enough; his drinking had become an every-night affair.

Finally he began going in the front door of the machine shop where he worked, punching the time clock and walking through the building and out the back door to a tavern just across the tracks, for a "belt" or two to get him through the day. Then he would go back in and go to work. He worked fast and well for all his drinking, and if his boss knew of his daily morning walk he never acknowledged it.

It got to the point where he couldn't sleep at night unless he knew he had enough left at bedtime for a good stiff drink in the morning. Many times he would be so sick in the morning that the drink wouldn't stay down, but with hands shaking so badly that he could scarcely hold a small drink in a large glass without spilling it, he would keep trying until he finally managed to hold the whisky down.

His need for alcohol was gradually building up, until

the time eventually came that he was to require a drink every two hours.

Speedy learned every job he ever tackled quickly and well—yet he was basically insecure, and always desperately afraid he couldn't make the grade. It was a vicious circle. He lost jobs because he drank—and his drinking increased as his confidence in himself waned.

It was while he was working for a dairy company that the first symptoms of his mental deterioration began to manifest themselves. Often now, lying on the couch, he would reach out to pat a dog that wasn't there. His driving became erratic, and he recalls how on one occasion he felt an almost uncontrollable urge to jump from his milk truck, and had to grip the steering wheel hard and force the thought from his mind in order to refrain from jumping.

That same night he was to walk into his house, apparently cold sober, and demand to see his mother. She had been dead for fifteen years.

And now his personality began to undergo a drastic change. He turned against people he had formerly liked, and insulted everyone who came to the house, until finally no one came, not even his own relatives.

One night Speedy jumped up from the supper table, accused his fifteen-year-old stepson Bill of looking at him in a queer fashion, and began to strike the boy with both fists. Bill ran upstairs with his father in pursuit, and Kay jumped between them. Speedy grabbed her by the throat and started choking her.

"His eyes were staring," she remembers, "and I know he didn't even see me. Instead of struggling, I let myself go limp and he finally let go, but not before he had choked the breath out of me."

This episode frightened Speedy as badly as it did his wife, and at last he seemed willing to seek help.

Going to the Red Cross which had helped him while he was in the service, he was advised to admit himself to the Receiving Hospital in Youngstown, Ohio.

It was not until he was inside the building that he realized he was in a mental hospital.

Enraged at being held there, he prevailed upon Kay's better judgment to secure his release. At the end of five weeks he was taken home against the urgent recommendation of his psychiatrist who warned that his condition was serious, and his alcoholism probably incurable.

It didn't take Kay long to realize her mistake. "If I thought he was bad before," she says, "I hadn't seen anything until now. Speedy would leave for work morning after morning, only to get as far as the first tavern. He would come home later in the day, blind drunk.

"Every night he would beg for another chance, and every morning I'd pack his lunch, only to have him throw it away and come home reeling. He soon lost his job and we had to go to the Soldiers Relief for help.

A social worker tried desperately but unsuccessfully to get Speedy back on his feet. He was doctoring with a well-known Warren physician who worked with him hard and long, but finally gave him up as a hopeless case.

He tried Alcoholics Anonymous and through this organization got a job with a steel company, where his employer was a member of AA—but it wasn't long before he went completely to pieces there. Screaming for his friends at work to hold him down, they finally took him to the AA hospital with D.T.'s.

The maximum stay allowable in this institution was

five days—for the hospital exists only for the purpose of drying out the patient and getting him back on his feet. The Veterans Administration Hospital would no longer admit him unless his wife probated him through the court, so that he could not get out once he was signed in.

For the first time George Speedy seemed to fully recognize the desperation of his plight, and he willingly acceded to his wife's and sister's suggestion that he go to Pittsburgh to take the Keeley Cure for alcoholism.

He drank all the way to Pittsburgh, where his sister who lived there, met him. She took him straight to the physician at Shadyside Hospital, for the medical examination always necessary before taking the cure. The doctor reported him to be in the last stages of alcoholism—his condition so desperate that he could never hope to survive the cure.

Over Speedy's violent protestations, for he had been two hours without alcohol and was craving a drink, he was admitted immediately into Shadyside Hospital and put to bed. Two hours later, the nurse making her rounds found the bed empty. An alarm was sent out and Speedy was finally found wandering around on the top floor in his hospital gown, suffering from hallucinations. He was put back in his own bed, but by now he had gone completely berserk.

He was strapped down to his hospital bed, with leather straps on his ankles, waist and wrists. Completely out of his mind, he was so violent and pulled so hard on the straps that they dug deep into his flesh until he bled.

"Until that time," Speedy says, "I always thought the talk about people having D.T.'s and seeing snakes was just a story, but believe me, it's true, and the snakes are absolutely real to you when you see them.

"That night I saw those snakes—chewing into my wrists and ankles and making them bleed. I remember screaming for someone to take them off me, and nobody paid any attention."

For six days Speedy lay strapped down. He recalls now, and still with horror, how he seemed to be living on a strip of earth between two rivers with a high cliff on each side. Now the snakes continually crawled out of the rivers, biting him—while Satan, black as midnight, stood on one cliff laughing fiendishly, and on the other sat many people, all sitting in pews as if in church. They were not talking or moving—just looking.

"I cried and cursed and begged for someone to help," relates Speedy, "but the devil just kept on laughing, and the 'church people' just kept on sitting and looking."

This sequence, which went on for so long, was the most terrifying of all his experiences. When he was finally discharged from the hospital, he felt lost and completely without hope—for far from being cured, he was now classified as definitely incurable, and warned that if he ever took another drink, it would cost him his life.

He could hardly wait to get out—not so he could see his family but so he could get a drink. Half an hour after he left the hospital, he was in a tavern.

During the next week at home, he was extremely fearful and deeply melancholy.

During one of his spells of melancholia, he had been upstairs for a long time—so long that his wife went up to investigate. She found him sitting on the edge of the bed with his head in his hands—and noticed immediately that the shotgun was gone from the corner by his bed.

She dared not let him know how terrified she felt, but sat down beside him, talking quietly and rubbing his arms soothingly with one hand while feeling under the bed with the other.

Her hand touched the gun, and she began easing it out slowly while she kept talking and patting his arm, until she persuaded him to lie down. When he was quiet and his eyes were closed, Kay picked up the gun, holding it horizontally against the side turned away from his so he wouldn't see it if he opened his eyes. All the while she prayed silently that she would be able to get downstairs before he missed her.

As soon as she was safely down, she removed the bolt and hid it—and just in time—for a second later Speedy came staggering down.

He begged and pleaded for the bolt, for he felt he was going into the D.T.'s again and said he would rather die now than go through that again. He hunted and hunted for the bolt but never found it. For days he carried two shotgun shells in his pocket, still asking and searching for the bolt.

"On more than one night," his wife recalls, "he made me tie his hands to the bed, he was so sure he was going berserk again, and so fearful of what he might do."

Life seemed to present a hopelessly grim picture for the Speedys. The husband, a hopeless and dangerous alcoholic; his wife's health badly damaged from the years of nervous tension she had undergone; no money except for the Soldiers' Relief check, and no one to whom they could turn for help.

Kay's family had done all they could, but their patience had come to an end, and they urged her to leave her husband, but Kay still loved him and simply couldn't abandon him. What would become of him if she left? His parents were dead; his sister and brother were afraid to have him in their homes; and the doctor's only recommendation was to permanently institutionalize him. The final blow seemed to have been struck when even their pastor refused to come and see him any more.

"Only the Lord was left to help me," says Kay, "and it almost seemed as if He were turning a deaf ear."

And then she took a part-time job—two or three hours a day caring for a little lady crippled with arthritis. Little did Kay know that this job was to prove, in a very real sense, a steppingstone to Speedy's salvation.

"Have you ever listened to Kathryn Kuhlman on the radio?" asked Miss Minor from her wheelchair, on the first day Kay reported to work.

"No," said Kay, as the question went in one ear and out the other.

But every day, with the regularity of clockwork came the same question: "Did you listen to Kathryn today?"

"I got so tired of saying 'no,' I decided I'd listen so I could say 'yes' for a change," says Kay, "*And what a change!* Her program hit me like a bolt out of the blue."

The very first time she listened, she heard the testimony of a former alcoholic, and for the first time in years real hope flared again within her. If Christ had delivered someone like Speedy, maybe—just maybe—Speedy could be helped, too.

With renewed and ever-increasing faith, she listened now each day to the program—on her knees throughout the broadcasts.

At about this time the Speedys moved into a "capped"

cellar which Kay's folks had built, planning to erect a house on the site five miles from town.

There was water and elecrtricity and a sink in the cellar, and that was all—no partitions, no other plumbing—but they paid no rent, and were grateful for a place to live.

Kay had hoped that living in the country would help Speedy—for with no car it would be difficult for him to get to town and to a bar, but somehow he always managed, sometimes walking five miles and often hitch-hiking.

Where he got the money for the drinks after he got there, no one seemed to know, for he always had enough for a couple and then someone would buy him a few more.

He had reached the point now that he was in a half stupor most of the time. The shakes were so bad, he could hardly hold a glass or a cup. He ate virtually nothing, and began each day with a drink of raw vinegar or vanilla extract.

Kay was on the verge of a nervous breakdown by now, and all that kept her going were the religious broadcasts. One night, sick and exhausted, she came to the end of her rope. Her prayers had seemed unavailing—for some reason God wasn't helping. "I decided that night that I would have to leave Speedy—forget God—and make a life of my own," she said. *"And then Christ's words came so clearly, it seemed He must have spoken aloud: 'And what will you do when trouble comes? For it will come— nothing's changed, and you can't forget Speedy in his desperate need just by walking away. Who will you turn to for help then?' "*

His words were all Kay needed.

"Without His strength," she says, "I knew I couldn't

have lived through even one day of the nightmare my life had been for so long. I made my decision that night to trust Him all the way—and then and there, I turned Speedy over to Him, lock, stock, and barrel—vowing I'd never fight with him again about his drinking, but be as kind and understanding as possible, and leave all the rest to God.

"That must have been what the Lord was waiting for me to do," she continued, "for the very next day there was the testimony on Kathryn's radio program which was to lead indirectly to Speedy's conversion."

The testimony was that of four one-time alcoholics, all of whom had been instantly delivered from liquor, and they were from Warren, a few miles from where the Speedys lived.

Kay was so excited she fell over herself, grabbing for pencil and paper to write down their names and telephone numbers. Within five minutes she was talking to one of them—Paul Winyard. How she prayed now that she could get Speedy to go to see Paul! Her prayer was answered, for surprisingly enough, Speedy agreed to go that very afternoon. It took him four hours to get there, for there were taverns along the way. But he finally made it—the worse for wear, but still able to absorb what Paul had to say. That night all four of the Warren men came out and told Speedy of their experiences. It was a thrilling thing to hear and Speedy said, "If the Lord did that for you guys, maybe there's hope for me." This was Friday night, and the next service was Sunday. Speedy excitedly agreed to go.

The next day, Saturday, he took off on an all-day drunk. It looked discouraging, but he finally returned home late Saturday night—very drunk, but still planning to go to the service the next morning.

He was up and ready early Sunday, with a terrible hangover, and shaking like a leaf, but all set to go when the Warren men called for him, well armed with spirits of ammonia should he need it.

Because of the large crowd, they had gone early to make sure of getting seats—so they had an hour to wait before the service actually began. Speedy was becoming very restless, and kept going outside, but each time he got up, one of the "gang" got up and went with him to make sure he didn't take off for good.

And then the service began.

"When you called me up to the altar, I wanted to run out the back door," Speedy recounts. "I was in bad shape—shaking so hard I could hardly stand. Remember, I had to have a drink every two hours to keep going at all. Well, now I had been in the auditorium for over three hours without one. I was falling to pieces, and I didn't have much faith that anything was going to happen to me. And then I thought, 'This is what I came here for, and it's now or never, my only chance.' "

So Speedy, head hanging as usual, went to the front of the Hall with three thousand people watching (and he could never stand crowds).

"I felt mighty small," he recalls, "When you told me to get down there on my knees, I did. And you prayed with me, and such an intense prayer it was, something I felt rather than heard. And I prayed too, and asked the Lord to forgive me. I remember how you pounded me on the shoulders as you prayed, emphasizing every word while the sweat poured off me like rain.

"This was the first time in my life," Speedy continued, "that I ever felt there had been a big burden lifted from me. As soon as I got up from my knees, I knew that something had happened. I knew that I would never want another drink again—that I had been delivered."

He had, indeed—from that moment on.

When he rose to his feet, he looked like a different person. He held his head high; his face was calm and joy shone from his eyes. His shaking had entirely stopped. It was a very long service lasting nearly six hours, and when Communion was served later in the day to that crowd of over three thousand people, Speedy sat with his tiny glass of grape juice filled almost to the brim—his hand now so steady he never spilled a drop. This was the same man who for so long had had to put his "shot" in the bottom of a water glass to keep it from slopping out.

This was the man who had gone into D. T.'s at Shadyside after less than three hours without a drink. This was the man who doctors said would be thrown into violent D.T.'s if all alcohol were to be suddenly withdrawn.

This was the man, his body "hopelessly" wrecked, his brain badly damaged by alcohol, who now stood erect and free—now an heir of God and a joint-heir with Christ Jesus—instantaneously and completely delivered from liquor.

His mental condition was completely cured, his physical body wholly restored; and he looked twenty years younger than when he had knelt a few minutes before, asking forgiveness of the Lord.

This is what the Son of the living God will do for a man or woman: this is the result of the greatest power in heaven and earth.

"The Lord knew He had to deliver me from alcohol," says Speedy, "for I had no will power of my own. If he hadn't taken the desire from me, I could never have made it."

Twelve years have passed—years filled with joy for the Speedys, as they live their lives dedicated to God— seeking to glorify Him in all they do.

Those whom God heals, *stay* healed—and from that day to this, Speedy has not had the slightest need or desire for a drink; nor would he think of "letting the Lord down" by ever taking one.

Within a few short months after his deliverance, Speedy had won the love of his children and gained the respect and admiration of all who knew or met him.

He had also won their *trust*—and his credit rating, which had been zero, now became A-1—as he discovered when they went to buy their home, and the bank checked his past record. For a while, their chances for a loan looked slim, indeed. And then a bank official, who knew all about Speedy and his conversion, stood up and vouched for him.

"It's hard to describe how much it means," says Speedy, "to have the respect and trust of your fellow man when you have never had it before."

Wherever he works as a construction man, from Ohio to Florida to South Dakota, he is well liked and does a superlatively good job.

One of his most recent jobs has been in the construction of a missile site in South Dakota—a job entailing great responsibility and dependability. During the job Speedy and his wife lived in the garden house of South Dakota's Senator E.C. Murray, doing yard work and many other chores for the senator, in exchange for their rent.

Possibly Speedy's proudest moment came when the senator wrote: "George is always a gentleman, and he is not only dependable but has considerable ability to do most anything. We like him and his wife very much, and we hope they see fit to continue with us for some time to come."

Speedy is proud of this letter, yes—but never for one moment does he forget the one to whom all the credit is due.

The greatest miracle in the world is the transformation of a life, when, literally, "if any man be in Christ, he is a new creature: old things are passed away; behold, all things are become new" (II Cor. 5:17).

The chemists of the Gulf Oil Company are able to take the black, dirty, filthy, stinking residue of the refinery and make it into pure, white, transparent paraffin—that is the ingenuity of man, coupled with the power of science.

But neither man nor science can take a human heart that is black with sin and make it clean and pure; man cannot take a human character that is besmirched and befouled with the pollution of Satan, and transform that life into a mighty instrument for righteousness. It takes a divine power; it takes God to make that transformation!

Environment, the power of the mind, the power of the will—all can do wonders, so far as they are able to go, but they can go just so far, and no further.

No power of man, and no man who is an alcoholic, has enough power of will strong enough to stop drinking instantly—with no desire for liquor thereafter—an instantaneous and permanent deliverance!

Medical science would also verify the fact, that if the

human body has been saturated with alcohol for years, to quit instantly could be such a shock to the human system, that the body could not stand it. That is why when one takes the "cure" it is usually a process of "tapering off."

Yet God can take a man and give to that man a spiritual healing, where he will experience an instantaneous deliverance, and actually be a "new person in Christ Jesus!"

It takes someone who is more than a man to redeem humanity like that! Try to explain such marvelous transformation of human character apart from the mighty power of the Holy Spirit; try to explain such deliverance apart from the miracle-working power of Jesus Christ, and you do violence to reason, and pour contempt upon the name and person of Christ who saved them.

23

What is the Key?

A *little* knowledge and an overabundance of zeal always tends to be harmful. In the area involving religious truths, it can be disastrous.

Not long ago, a well-meaning person painted my portrait in oils. To the artist it was a masterpiece, but our radio announcer who happened to be in the office as I was unwrapping the picture, took one look, and in his quiet way, commented, "An overabundance of good intentions, but no talent!"

Often I am prone to react in exactly the same way to those who have so much to say about faith, those who profess to be authorities on the subject, who claim to have all the answers regarding faith healing, even to the point of judging those who fail to receive healing from the giving hand of God.

In the early part of my ministry, I was greatly disturbed over much that I observed occurring in the field of divine healing. I was confused by many of the "methods" I saw employed, and disgusted with the unwise "performances" I witnessed—none of which I could associate in any way with either the action of the Holy Spirit or, indeed, the very nature of God.

Too often I had seen pathetically sick people dragging their tired, weakened bodies home from a healing service, having been told that they were not healed simply because of their own lack of faith. My heart ached for these people, as I knew how they struggled, day after day, trying desperately to obtain more faith, taking out that which they had, and trying to analyze it, in a hopeless effort to discover its deficiency which was presumably keeping them from the healing power of God. And I knew the inevitability of their defeat, because they were unwittingly looking at themselves, rather than to God.

But what *was* the answer? Again and again I was to ask myself the question: why were some healed and others not? Was there no balm in Gilead?

Was faith something that one could manufacture, or work up in oneself? Was it something that could be obtained through one's own goodness or moral status? Was it something that could be procured in exchange for serving the Lord, or through benevolence? I knew God could not lie, for He had promised; I knew in my own heart that there *was* healing, for I had seen the evidence from those who had been healed. It was real, and it was genuine, but *what was the key?*

I could not see the hand of God in man's superfluity of zeal and I saw the harm that was being done in attributing everything to "lack of faith" on the part of the individual who had not received his healing. Inside myself, I was crushed: my heart told me that God could do anything; my mind told me that through ignorance and lack of spiritual knowledge, there were those who were bringing a reproach on something that was sacred and wonderful and accessible to all. No preacher had to tell me that the power of God was real and that God knew no such thing as a MIRACLE as such, for I was assured by these facts as I read the Word of God. The Word was there, the promise had been given: there was surely no changing of God's mind, and certainly no canceling of the promise!

I think that no one has ever wanted a truth more avidly than I—nor sought it harder.

I remember well the evening when I walked from under a big tent where a divine healing service was being conducted. The looks of despair and disappointment on the faces I had seen, when told that only their lack of faith was keeping them from God, was to haunt me for weeks.

Was this, then, the God of all mercy and great compassion? I remember that night how, with tears streaming down my face, I looked up and cried; "They have taken away my Lord and I know not where they have laid Him." And I remember going to my room and sobbing out my heart to God—praying for light on the truth.

Fortunately I had learned a valuable spiritual lesson early in my ministry—one which was to come to my aid now: I had learned that the only way to get the truth is to come in sincerity and absolute honesty of heart and mind, and let the Lord Himself give one the blessed revelations of His Word, and *through* the Word, make His Presence real and His truth known.

At no time in my search did I profess to wear the robe of infallibility. I did not seek as a dogmatist, nor as one with a closed mind, but only as one who was daily learning, willing to be guided by the Holy Spirit, and longing to be taught of the Father—as one who was hungry for deeper spiritual knowledge, not from man but from *God.*

I waited expectantly for the answer, and it came.

One night during a series of services that I was conducting, a very fine Christian lady arose from where she was sitting in the audience and said, "Please—before you begin your sermon, may I give a word of testimony regarding something that happened last evening while you were preaching?"

I nodded, and quickly recalled what I had said the night before. There had not been anything unusual about the sermon: it had been a very simple message regarding the person of the Holy Spirit. I clearly recalled the sum and substance of the message.

God the Father is seated on His throne, and is the Giver of every good and perfect gift. At His right Hand is His Son, through whom we receive salvation and healing for our bodies, and in whom every need of our lives is met. The Holy Spirit is the only member of the Trinity who is here on earth and working in conjunction with the Father and the Son. He is here to do anything for us that Jesus would do, were He here in person.

I listened now, as the little woman spoke:

"As you were preaching on the Holy Ghost," she said, "telling us that in Him lay the resurrection power, I felt the power of God flow through my body. Although not a word had been spoken regarding the healing of the sick, I knew instantly and definitely that my body had been

226

healed. So sure was I of this, that I went to the doctor today and had my healing verified."

The Holy Spirit, then, was the answer: an answer so profound that no human being can fathom the full extent of its depths and power, and yet so simple that most folks miss it!

I understood that night why there was no need for a healing line; no healing virtue in a card or a personality; no necessity for wild exhortations "to have faith."

That was the beginning of this healing ministry which God has given to me; strange to some because of the fact that hundreds have been healed just sitting quietly in the audience, without any demonstration whatsoever, and even without admonition. This is because the presence of the Holy Spirit has been in such abundance that by His Presence alone, sick bodies are healed, even as people wait on the outside of the building for the doors to open.

Many have been the times when I have felt like taking the shoes off my feet, knowing that the ground on which I stood was holy ground. Many are the times when the power of the Holy Ghost is so present in my own body that I have to struggle to remain on my feet. Many are the times when His very Presence healed sick bodies before my eyes; my mind is so surrendered to the Spirit, that I know the exact body being healed: the sickness, the affliction, and in some instances, the very sin in their lives. And yet I could not pretend to tell you *why or how!*

From the beginning, as now, I was wholly sure of two things: first, that I had nothing to do with what was happening, and second, I *knew* that it was the supernatural power of Almighty God. I have been satisfied to leave the why and the how to Him, for if I knew the

227

answers to those two questions, then I would be God!

In the light of God's great love, tenderness and compassion, the Holy Spirit revealed to me my worthlessness and helplessness of self. His greatness was overwhelming; I was only a sinner, saved by the grace of God. The power was His and the glory and this glory, *His* glory, He will not share with any human being.

If you can once grasp the concept of the Holy Trinity, many things which may once have puzzled you become clear. The three persons of the Trinity, God the Father, God the Son and God the Holy Ghost are a unity. They are co-existent—infinite and eternal. All three were equally active in the work of creation, and are equally active and indispensible in the work of redemption. But although the three work together as one, each has at the same time His own distinctive function.

God the Father planned and purposed the creation and the redemption of man, and is "the Big Boss." God the Son provided and purchased at Calvary what the Father had planned in eternity. He made possible the realization of God's eternal plan. All that we receive from the Father *must* come through Jesus Christ the Son, and that is why at the heart of our faith is a Person—the very Son of the very God. When we pray, we come before the Father's throne in Jesus' Name. We cannot obtain an audience with the Father, except as we come to Him in the name of His Son.

But the Holy Spirit is the *power* of the Trinity. It was *His* power which raised Jesus from the dead. It is that *same* Resurrection power that flows through our physical bodies today, healing and sanctifying.

In short, when we pray in the Name of Jesus, the Father

looks down through the complete perfection, the utter holiness, the absolute righteousness of His only begotten Son, knowing that by Him, the price was paid in full for man's redemption, and *in* Him, lies the answer to every human need.

God honors the redemptive work of His Son by giving to us through Him, the desire of our hearts. Thus, while it is the Resurrection power of the Holy Spirit which performs the actual healing of the physical body, Jesus made it perfectly clear that we are to look to Him, the Son, in faith, for He is the One who has made all these things possible.

FAITH

Volumes have been written and volumes more have been spoken regarding this indefinable something called *faith,* and yet in the final analysis we actually know so little of the subject.

Faith is that quality or power by which the things desired become the things possessed. This is the nearest to a definition of faith attempted by the inspired Word of God.

You cannot weigh it or confine it to a container: it is not something you can take out and look at and analyze: you cannot definitely put your finger on it and positively say, "this is it." To explain it precisely and succinctly is almost like trying to define energy in one comprehensive statement. In the realm of physics we are told that the atom is a world within itself, and that the potential energy contained within this tiny world is such that it bewilders the mind of the average person. Attempt to define it, and you will run into difficulties. And so it is with faith in the realm of the spirit. But although it is not easy to define exactly what faith *is,* we know what it is *not.*

One of the most common errors we make in this regard is to confuse faith with presumption. We must be constantly alert to the danger of mistaking one for the other, for there is a vast difference between the two.

There is a pebble on the beach, for example, but the beach is more than the pebble. When the pebble asserts that it is the beach, then we say to it: "You are assuming too much."

There are many who mix the ingredients of their own mental attitude with a little confidence, a pinch of trust and a generous handful of religious egotism. They proceed to add some belief, along with many other ingredients, and mixing it in a spiritual apothecary's crucible, they label the total result *faith.* Actually, the consequence of this heterogeneous mixture is more likely to be presumption than faith.

Faith is more than belief; it is more than confidence; it is more than trust, and above all, it is never boastful. If it is pure faith, Holy Ghost faith, it will never work contrary to the Word of God, and neither will it work contrary to His wisdom and will.

There have been times when I have felt faith so permeate every part of my being, that I have dared to say and do things which, had I leaned to my own understanding or reason, I would never have done. Yet it flowed through every word and act with such irresistible power that I literally stood in wonder at the mighty works of the Lord. One thing I know: in you and in me apart from God, there are *no* ingredients and *no* qualities which, however mixed or combined, will create even so much as a mustard seed of Bible faith.

Let us just reason together in a very simple way: if I wanted to cross a lake, and there were no means of getting across except by boat, the sensible thing for me to do would be to secure a boat. It would be most foolish for me to seek the other side of the lake, when I needed to seek the proper conveyance to get there. Get the boat, and it will take you there.

Now, where do we get the faith that will take us across the lake? The answer to this question is positive and sure!

Faith is a gift of God or a fruit of the Spirit, and whether it be gift or fruit, the source and the origin of faith remain the same. It comes from God and is a gift of God.

If your faith is powerless, it is not faith. You cannot have faith without results any more than you can have motion without movement. The thing we sometimes call faith is only trust, but although we trust in the Lord, it is *faith* which has action and power.

A man might well trust the Lord and His promise that some day he would be saved and that some day he would accept Christ in the forgiveness of his sins: he might well trust the Lord sufficiently to believe that God had the ability to forgive his sins. But it is only if this man possesses an active, power-filled faith for salvation that he can be "born again."

"By grace are ye saved, through faith, and that not of yourselves; it is the gift of God" (Eph. 2:8,9).

Grace and faith are so closely related that you cannot separate one from the other. The wonder of it all is the fact that many times, faith is imparted when we feel the least deserving. But faith is not the product of merit, for no human being deserves salvation, and no person living merits the smallest of God's blessings: that is why the two, grace and faith, are so closely related.

The faith imparted to the sinner for salvation is solely the result of God's mercy and grace. It is a gift. The faith that is imparted to the individual for the healing of his physical body is again only the result of God's mercy; the overflow of His great compassion and grace. It is a gift. You do not pray for faith; you seek the Lord, and faith will come.

The disciples and the Master were on the waters of Galilee. It was a beautiful day; the lake was calm and serene, and there was scarcely a cloud in the sky—when suddenly, a terrific storm arose! The poor disciples were terror stricken. The wind was blowing in all its fury, the little boat was about to capsize, and they were certain that their very lives were at stake.

Finally in desperation, they awakened the sleeping Christ. Calmly, without perturbation, He asked just one question: "Where is your faith?" (Luke 8:25).

Where was it? Had they left it on shore before entering the boat? Had it dropped to the depth of the sea on which their little boat was sailing? Had it fled on the shoulders of the storm?

Their faith had been resting in the stern of the boat!

Their faith was with them all the time: it had never left them for one second. *He* was their faith; but the mistake they had made was in forgetting the fact of His Presence, while discerning the fact of the storm! That is exactly what Jesus meant when He said, "without me ye can do nothing." *He,* then, is your faith.

We become defeated when we fasten our eyes on circumstances, our own problems, our weaknesses, our physical illnesses. The surest way in the world to be defeated is to focus our mind on ourselves. The storm will capsize our little boat, of that we can be sure, and yet, the fact remains that our faith for victory was nearer to us than our hands or feet.

No person need ever be defeated on a single score; no person needs to lack faith. Look up, as Carey Reams did, and see Jesus! He is your faith, He is our faith. It is not faith that you must seek, *but Jesus.*

The Giver of every good and perfect gift is the Author and Finisher of our faith!

I BELIEVE

I believe that the Holy Bible is the Word of the living God; that it is the supernaturally inspired Word; that it was written by holy men of old as they were moved and inspired by the Holy Ghost; that it is the only true ground of Christian unity and fellowship. That it is the eternal tribunal by whose standards all men, and nations shall be judged.

I believe in the Trinity: Father, Son and Holy Ghost, as three separate individuals; equal in every divine perfection.

I believe in God the Father Almighty, Creator of heaven and earth, whose glory is so exceedingly bright that mortal men cannot look upon His face and live. His nature so transcends human standards of comparison that a definition is impossible. Faith begins where reason and logic ends!

I believe that Jesus Christ is the very Son of the living

God, co-existent and co-eternal with the Father, who was conceived by the Holy Ghost and born of the Virgin Mary. He took upon Himself the form of man, and by the shedding of His blood, made atonement for fallen man.

Just as prophecy is the unanswerable argument in the realm of external evidence, so the Person of Jesus Christ is the unanswerable argument in the realm of internal evidence. Not only does His entire life fulfill perfectly the Old Testament prophecies, but His Person, towering as it does above every other, is beyond explanation only as we admit Him to be very God as well as very man.

The miraculous life of Christ is an unanswerable argument for His miraculous birth!

I believe the Holy Spirit is a person, and a divine person, and not just a divine influence. The marks of personality are knowledge, feeling and will, and any being who knows, thinks, feels and wills, is a person whether he has a body or not. All the distinctive marks or characteristics of personality are ascribed to the Holy Spirit in the Word.

As a member of the eternal Trinity, the Holy Ghost has aided in the creation of the earth and its forms of life. He was present at the creation of man. Hence the words: "Let *us* make man."

I believe that by voluntary disobedience and transgression, man fell from innocence and purity, to the depths of sin and iniquity.

Because of man's fallen state, judgments had to be met, law had to be satisfied, penalties had to be paid; all of these things the holiness of God required.

Jesus Christ the Son, through the Holy Ghost, offered

Himself to God the Father as a propitiation for sin; that is why Christ is referred to as "The lamb slain from the foundation of the world."

The blood of Christ is so effective that it not only cleanses from all sin, but one day the effect of that blood shed in Jerusalem nineteen hundred years ago will remove the curse of sin from the earth.

His sinless blood is a sufficient atonement for our sin!

I believe in salvation as a *definite* experience—an experience through which the individual is no longer under the bondage of sin, but "is passed from death unto life," transformed by the Power of the Spirit. Quite literally "a new creature in Christ Jesus."

By simple faith, belief in God's Son, and acceptance of Him as divine Saviour, the guilty sinner is made righteous.

I believe in that "called out" body of believers, composed of Jew and Gentile, and individuals from every kindred, people, tribe and nation, originating at Pentecost, and known as "The Body of Christ."

I believe that the only way Jesus, who is now at the right hand of God, as Great High Priest, can manifest Himself to the world is through His Body, the Church.

I believe that this Body, comprised of those who have been washed in the shed blood of the Son of God, is to be the Bride of Christ and will reign with Him in His millennial glory.

I BELIEVE IN MIRACLES!